P9-CBI-993

ANTHROPOLOGISTS
and What They Do

ANTHROPOLOGISTS
and What They Do

by

Margaret Mead

FRANKLIN WATTS, INC.
575 Lexington Avenue, New York 10022

FIRST PRINTING

Library of Congress Catalog Card Number: 65–15076
Printed in the United States of America

ACKNOWLEDGMENTS

I wish to thank my eighteen colleagues whose interviews appear in this book. I wish also to thank Mario Bick, May Ebihara Gelfand, Karen Hunter, Warren Lane, Beatrice Peach, Roger Peranio, Gertrude Pinsky, Barbara Price, Anne Howland Russell, Constance Sutton, Helga Wolff, and particularly Milly Salwen for their help in the preparation of this book.

The author and publisher wish to thank the U.S. National Museum for permission to reproduce a passage from Franz Boas' "The Social Organization and the Secret Societies of the Kwakiutl Indians," *Report of the U.S. National Museum for the Year Ending June 30, 1895,* pages 419–20, and William Morrow & Co., Inc. for permission to reprint pages 14–19 from *Coming of Age in Samoa,* by Margaret Mead, Copyright © 1928, 1955 by Margaret Mead.

MARGARET MEAD

The American Museum of Natural History
New York
July 10, 1964

Contents

ANTHROPOLOGISTS
and What They Do

I

Anthropology Is Fieldwork

Anthropologists are, above all, men and women who like to work with living people, with spoken languages rather than languages that have been written down, and with the real things that ancient peoples made—their tools, weapons, and pots, and the foundations of their houses.

We like the people and the things we study to be in their natural settings—Eskimos at home in the Arctic; South Sea islanders on South Sea islands, native speakers in their own villages, talking to each other, making speeches, and telling stories where they can ask the old woman next door for the details they have forgotten. We like to do our own digging for the remains of earlier civilizations, making diagrams and photographs as we go along.

Most of all we like to spend our lives on field trips, away from offices and laboratories and storerooms, out somewhere collecting new materials, making new photographs, learning new languages. There is always the temptation to take a new field trip before the last one has been properly written up, and to put off until later the tedious task of classifying what we have already brought home from the field. The mere suggestion that a new field trip may be possible sets an anthropologist to sniffing the air for the remembered smells of fish oil, copra, roasting tapir, burning charcoal, or chewed betel nut.

Instead of merely describing what anthropologists do, my natural inclination is to set up a field trip, a special field trip for high-school students who want to know what anthropology is about. On such a trip, I would like to bring all the students who are interested in anthropology into The American Museum of Natural History where they could talk with my colleagues, and up to Columbia University where they could talk with the professors and students.

I would like to take the students around the country to the different kinds of places where anthropologists do research and apply their knowledge—in hospitals; in departments of health; in special laboratories where they are making films or analyzing recordings of music; in government departments where they are acting as advisers on such matters as technical assistance, educational programs for peoples newly coming into the modern world, or relations with other countries.

I would also like them to have a chance to go to the field—to Western New Guinea where the Harvard expedition made the film *Dead Birds;* to the wilds of Borneo where Tom Williams and Bob and Diane Harrison are working among the Dusun; to the Arctic where Asen Balikci (who came to us from Turkey) is making a film on the Eskimo; or to southeastern Mexico where John Gwaltney, a blind student, is studying a village of people, most of whom have gone blind. Or they might go to the little towns in northern Washington where the old Indians still remember the tales of Mink and Coyote and the troubles they got themselves into; or to France where Julian Pitt-Rivers is slowly gaining an understanding of his French neighbors by working his own farm.

In actual fact, however, a field tour with students would be impractical. Fieldwork is not suitable for crowds. Usually it is done by one man or one woman alone or by a man and his wife working together. Sometimes a small team may go to the field, a team of archeologists, for example, who are digging and who get to know the living people mainly as workers on the dig, or a team of anthropologists who are making a film or gathering a collection for a museum. But in face-to-face work with people, a busload of eager questioners (or even quiet *looklooks,* as the New Guinea people call observers) will not do. Only by going out in two's or three's could students get a feeling for what a real field trip is like.

Since this is so, I have decided to construct the kind

of field trip that high-school students might really take, and to present anthropology in response to the kinds of questions they might ask. And instead of imagining a visit to some faraway field site, in Africa or in New Guinea, this will be a field trip to actual anthropologists at work.

In reading about anthropologists and their work, it is possible to think both of the near future, when there is still so much to be done by anthropologists, and the far future, when anthropologists' work will be very different. In that distant future—in our great-grandchildren's day—there will be no more primitive people living as they lived for thousands of years, no more buried cities to discover, no more unusual languages to record, no important missing links in the story of man's physical development. All they shall have then will be our records—written, filmed, and taped—of bygone ways of life, specimens of the tools men once used and the weapons they fought with, and models of the natural settings in which they lived.

But even then anthropologists will be needed. People trained in the way this knowledge can be used will be needed to help human beings live, without war, on one planet. Their knowledge will be needed to feed and clothe and shelter the billions of people living on earth, and it will be needed to help people rear their children in ways that will give them a better chance, each one to be what he has the potentiality to become.

These are projects for the far future, when anthropologists will have to be trained from the records. In the near future, the period when those who are high-school students today can make their contribution, we must hurry, hurry, hurry to get the records in before the last primitive man puts on clothes and starts paying taxes; before the last rich deposit of early civilization is flooded over by the waters of a vast new irrigation project or is dug up by little boys who do not know that they are destroying priceless relics; before the rare fascinating languages spoken by a handful of people in some remote valley are forgotten as they are displaced by the languages that will be broadcast from the Telstars of the future.

In the next quarter of a century, a tremendous amount of work must be done to rescue these vanishing traces of the past. Once the last primitive peoples enter the modern world—become members of one of the great religions, save their babies' lives with antibiotics, follow the world's news, and take part in its councils—there will be no way of ever finding out what their earlier life was like.

Without this record we shall have lost priceless information about what we might have been like ourselves, had the history of our own ancestors been only slightly different—had they (like the primitive peoples we know about) been shut off in little groups, away from the highways and seaways of the world and isolated from the inventions which each of the great civilizations has made and then spread to everyone within reach.

Primitive peoples leave no written records. They

are called "primitive" just because they do not share a civilization in which at least a few people know how to write. They build with mud and straw, with blocks of snow, or with small stones. Their languages perish when the last speaker dies—unless a linguist has recorded their living accents on a tape recorder. Their dances, intricate and lovely, perish too—unless the steps, which no one knows how to write down, have been recorded with a movie camera.

At this moment in history we have wonderful devices for measuring the age of bone and wood (by carbon fourteen and other methods based on modern physics), for locating archeological sites by air surveys. There is new sensitized film that can be used to take pictures in dark huts or on unlighted hillsides where primitive women still have their babies or where séances are held and men talk with ghosts and no lights are permitted. Film and tape can record the last primitive initiation ceremonies, the last primitive warfare.

Scientists in the future will need these records if they are to be trained to think broadly and deeply about men who, sharing a common basic biology, have yet learned to behave so differently in Chicago and Calcutta, in London and Tokyo and the Philippine Islands, in the Orkneys and Sardinia and Kazakhstan. If men in the future are to have the benefit of a knowledge of how men lived in the past, as they plan new kinds of cities on earth and new colonies in space, all this must be collected now.

Perhaps it is equally interesting to think about what it is that any period in history shares with any other, but I myself have always found it more interesting to ask: What is different about this period in which I live? What must be done now that can otherwise never be done at all?

II

The Museum

Any field trip constructed to show high-school students what anthropology is like must be based in an actual place at a particular time. I have chosen The American Museum of Natural History and Columbia University, both in New York City, because these are the places where I work, that I know well, and where I can most easily ask my colleagues to cooperate in making this a real field trip into anthropology in America today. If someone else were writing this book, the field trip could take place just as well in Chicago, or San Francisco, or Boston, or Philadelphia, or Columbus, Ohio. And I have chosen a single day in the Museum, which I shall write about in the "ethnographic present"—as if the things were happening today—because here, as in actual fieldwork, no two days are alike. In the Museum, some exhibits are permanent, arranged to stay, a few of them as long as a half-century ago; others are temporary, set up for only a few weeks to display a new find or a new contribution to the Museum's collections.

Entering the front door of the Museum on the morning I have in mind, you are immediately caught up in a stampede of schoolchildren, whose teachers are trying to keep them in groups, as they talk excitedly about dinosaurs, reptiles, fish, and Indians. You might expect somehow that anthropology would have a museum all to itself, perhaps with an exhibit of arrowheads that were dug up locally and a map showing where Indians once lived in this region. As you look around the great entrance hall, there is indeed a diorama of New York in about 1660, showing Peter Stuyvesant, the governor, receiving a delegation of Hackensack Indians from across the Hudson River. But through the far door you can glimpse some scenes showing North American mammals and, to the right, a diorama of marsh birds in flight at evening. Someone asks eagerly to see the fossil pterosaur, a flying reptile, found in April, 1961, by three tenth-grade boys in Granton Quarry, New Jersey. Someone else is clamoring to see the exhibit that shows in a cutaway section of the earth the seasonally changing activities of small animals that live underground.

Suddenly it becomes clear that anthropology is a

natural science, with its place among all the natural sciences based on fieldwork, and that anthropologists, like other natural scientists, go off on expeditions to study living creatures in their local habitat.

The Museum is the appropriate center of these activities. From the Museum, expeditions go out to study birds and fishes, insects and men, rocks and rivers, all with the same objective. The scientists go to the Himalayas, New Guinea, or the Canadian Rockies so that they can observe their subjects under natural conditions, making careful notes on everything that cannot be taken back, and gathering up samples of everything that can be studied, classified, and analyzed later. The materials can then be written up in scientific monographs and exhibited in meaningful ways, using photographs to reconstruct each detail of the place where they were found—the colors and shapes of the leaves and flowers, the kind of soil—so that schoolchildren and older students, looking at the exhibits, can more fully understand their place in their original settings.

In the main corridors, maps of every floor show the subject of each hall. Using these, visiting students can plan a route that will take them through many of the anthropological halls on their way up to the top-floor offices. Moving from the natural history to the anthropological exhibits and recognizing the relationships between them, students may have a sense of seeing with new eyes these reconstructions of men's ways of living.

What most people learn about science in high school

emphasizes laboratories and experiments. The scientist, as he is shown in movies or on television or in advertisements, is usually indoors, wearing a white lab coat, working with test tubes or beakers, and surrounded by different kinds of apparatus. In a biology class, the focus is often on dissecting. And social science classes spend a great deal of time discussing *the* family—with statistics about the age of marriage, the number of marriages that end in divorce, and the average number of children in middle-income homes—as if our kind of family was the only kind in the world.

The Museum offers another approach. Wandering through the halls, you may find that you have gained a new sense of freedom and movement as you look at the diorama of the forest community, showing the natural food web of the forest. Next to it you will see the exhibit of man and the land, beginning with an Algonquin Indian woman standing with her simple gardening tools and ending with the modern farmer in the midst of his complex, mechanized equipment. And around the bend you will catch a glimpse of a glorious autumn landscape.

Natural history means going outdoors—up mountains, to islands, up rivers, through forests, across high plateaus—to study things that are alive or, as in the case of dinosaur skeletons and the bones of early men, things that once were alive. Everywhere, even in the delicately patterned skulls of rodents that line a side corridor wall and in the frail and elegant pterosaur fossils embedded in limestone that are displayed in the dinosaur hall, there is this sense of life. This feeling of being in the midst of life is due to the care with which the habitat groups show total scenes—Indians making pottery, Eskimos using their dogsleds, villagers on a Pacific island working in the shade of their houses built up on stilts. In every scene the trees are right and the color of the sky, too. The relationship between men and other living things is maintained.

Within the walls of the Museum, you can experience all the seasons of the year, every continent, the struggle for existence, the world before man appeared on the scene, and man's first efforts to shape tools from stone and bone. Yet you are constantly reminded that this is indeed the mid-twentieth century, for there are exhibits that use the most modern theoretical approaches—to genetics, for example—and the techniques used in preparing the exhibits are modern, also.

New methods of dating old bone and other organic materials, based on nuclear physics, helped to work out the background for dating Neanderthal Man. Without the use of modern plastics and electronic recording, it would not have been possible to make the Transparent Woman, whose internal workings are shown in the Hall of the Biology of Man.

A special temporary exhibition of Peruvian art and life shows how careful work with the microscope and the most modern chemical analyses are used to reconstruct fragile, fading pieces of textiles and, through them, ancient ways of weaving.

In another hall, two preparators are working with

large photographs showing the different ways in which small babies are carried and the relationship between these positions and the ways they later stand and walk and talk. Here is an illustration of a point in theory about human behavior which has developed over the last twenty-five years into a new science, called kinesics.

In the Museum, the visitor has access to all the living world, moving back toward the beginning of time and onward into the future. Near the stairs there is a case with two sledges—one used by Robert E. Peary in his dash to the North Pole on April 6, 1909, and the other used by Roald Amundsen, the first explorer to reach the South Pole on December 14, 1911. Nowhere, for more than a few minutes, can one forget that man is part of nature, a living creature, hungry and thirsty, needing warmth and shelter to survive.

Finally, as visitors go past the sign that reads "No exhibits above this floor," and arrive at the working offices on the fifth floor, they may have a pleasant sense of going behind the scenes—as if they were about to see the wheels behind the face of some giant watch. Up here, on the curators' floor, the long halls are lined with tall wood and metal cabinets and the air has a curious smell—a little stale, a little chemical—a compound of fumigating substances and the mixed smells of actual specimens, bones, feathers, samples of soils, and minerals. Here and there some out-of-date specimen—a stuffed eagle on a wooden stand, an old-fashioned model of a chimpanzee—can be seen stored on top of a case. Walking along these halls, if you had come directly up to this floor, you could quite easily get a different idea of a museum as a place filled with specimens smelling of formaldehyde, all rather musty and dated and dead. There is no immediate sense of life.

But suddenly two men appear in the corridor, pushing a wheeled cart loaded with weapons, baskets, feathers—a fascinating jumble. And as they pass, one man remarks, "We'll never get Borneo done by May first!"

III

What Museum Curators Do

These are the interviews with some members of my department at the Museum. I explained the kind of book I was writing, and I asked them to imagine that they were talking to a group of high-school students. Some of them were better at doing this than others. Occasionally one of them would forget that his actual audience was not sitting across the desk from him, and he slipped into rather technical language. Ordinarily this kind of mismatching can easily be edited out. But it is a basic rule of fieldwork never to tamper with the record of what actually has been said, for one risks losing the authentic style and flavor of the informant's thinking. This is why the technical terms have been left in.*

I asked each of my colleagues the same three questions so that you may more easily compare their answers. This was necessary, you will find, because they do very many different kinds of things.

Anthropologists deal with everything about a people—what they look like; their physical measurements and blood types; where they came from; what they believe about their past; how they bring up their children; what they make and what they must buy from other people; what they sell and what they inherit; what they think of as beautiful and what they reject as ugly; and where they believe their souls go when they die.

Naturally, no anthropologist can be trained to be equally good at every kind of activity. It is possible to specialize in music or pottery designs, weapons or agricultural methods, religious beliefs or ideas of law, and still to take into account a people's whole way of life. You will find a great variety of interests and specialties in the interviews with the curators at the Museum and, in the next chapter, with the Columbia University professors.

Although the interviews were recorded in a given sequence and are arranged in this book in a particular order, this does not mean that you must follow the same order in reading them. When we design a hall in the Museum, we do not mark out pathways that

* Technical terms are explained in the glossary.

oblige the visitor to look at the exhibits in a specific sequence. Instead, we leave him free to wander and look at the things that interest him as long as he likes, skip other things, and choose for himself what he wants to see. Similarly, dipping and sampling is probably the best way to read the interviews that follow. It is harder to arrange for this in a book than in a museum hall, but anthropologists know that in a field report everything is needed at the same time. There is no chapter that should come first.

As a guide to the people, the places, and the topics that are most interesting to you, there is at the back of the book, in Appendix B, a brief description of each of the anthropologists interviewed—a *curriculum vitae.* Here you can find out when each one was born, what his training was, and something about his special interests and the parts of the world where he has worked. The pages of each interview are given there, so you can quickly find any one of them.

The offices in the Museum where these interviews were held are large high rooms, lined with cabinets and piled with books, as many offices are, but with this difference—each has its special collection of objects brought back from different parts of the world: drums, masks, bits of textile, war amulets, carvings, bark-cloth pounders. Each curator is responsible for one area of the world or else for one aspect of anthropology, such as archeology or physical anthropology; the objects in his office speak for his special interests.

A curator's office is a workshop. Here he spreads out

new specimens to catalogue or old ones to study. Here he makes selections for exhibits, comparing his field notes and his field photographs with objects collected on a recent field trip or perhaps a half-century ago. Here he also answers all kinds of questions over the telephone.

"Is there a Nuku Hiva language?"

"I'm doing a painting for the Phi Gam Club, and I have to paint a Fijian canoe. . . ." (If he is lucky, he may remember the old fraternity song, "That's how my Phi Gam spends his Fiji honeymoon.")

"I want to find an island where nobody has ever seen a fluorescent watch."

"What kind of bone did the people in West New Guinea use to make their arrow tips?"

Here in his office he also talks with people who bring in specimens they would like to have identified—two arrow points picked up in a plowed field during the campaign to liberate France during World War II; a piece of bark cloth carefully laid away in a trunk in Grandmother's attic; an old ivory carving that Grandfather brought back from a sea voyage.

And here in the Museum the anthropologist hopes and plans for his next field trip. He may have hung a real map of his destination on his office wall. Sometimes, when he has been a curator for many years, no wall space is left, but by this time he has his map in his head.

In each of these offices I sat down with my tape recorder and asked questions.

COLIN M. TURNBULL

October 18, 1961

This office is large and light. There is something about it that makes you think of the arts. Perhaps it is the group of African musical instruments lying on the table—strange in shape, but clearly meant for music.

What are you doing at this moment?

At this moment I'm writing some letters. Every morning there are a number of letters here from the public that have to be answered. General queries about Africa, in my case. And then there are also letters from other museums, universities . . .

What's that letter about?

It's from somebody who made a film for us recently in Africa. I helped him with the editing of it and we're now going over the script together, and I am writing to him confirming an appointment for the final viewing of this film.

What part of Africa was that?

That was Mozambique.

And how long did you stay there?

I was never there myself, but this particular person was out there for a couple of months.

Now, what is the most interesting thing you've done so far in your anthropological life?

Oh, I think without any doubt, the work that I did in the Belgian Congo. That was among the Pygmies. I spent some years there, on three separate trips.

You said you worked with Pygmies. How much smaller were they than you are?

About two feet.

Did you find it hard to work with them because they were that small?

No, not the slightest. I think the physical difficulties are the ones you get over the easiest.

Do you think of them as children?

Not the slightest.

Well, if you had to deal with a man who was two feet smaller than you were, would you think he thought you were a giant?

No, I don't think the size influenced them particularly favorably. They think of tall people, on the other hand, as being rather clumsy and as probably being rather stupid.

Oh, they do. Now, what other tall people do they meet?

The other African tribes round about are considerably taller than they are. The point is that the Pygmies are masters in *their* world. And this is really the exciting thing about fieldwork: we have to try to put ourselves in their position and see the world as they see it. And when we do this, we no longer think of them as children; in fact, we realize that *we* are the children because we know so little about their world.

What was the most interesting thing you found out about their world?

I think the intense—the very close—relationship that they have with the world around them. This is something I feel we have lost—many of us have lost—here. We live in a totally artificial world that we've built ourselves, and the real world around us, the earth and the sky—everything that makes it wonderful—we've just lost touch with it. And these were the most important things to these people: the forest, the trees, the rivers, the sun, which they very seldom saw—all these things were important to them. This was the real world to them. And they built up a wonderful religion around this belief in the world, this belief in the goodness of the world.

Have you written anything about them?

Yes, I wrote a book recently; it's called *The Forest People*.

Now, what's the most interesting thing you've done here at the Museum?

Oh, my heavens, almost anything one does here at the Museum is interesting.

Do you put on exhibits?

Yes, I have put on two exhibits. The first one was not entirely concerned with Africa. It was on musical instruments all around the world. The idea of that was to try to show what part music plays in human society; how different people use it; what it means to different people. And then, more recently, there was an exhibit of recent accessions from Africa. A number of people have given us some very beautiful pieces, and we put on an exhibit to show these pieces.

Did you do anything especially interesting in exposition techniques when you put on your musical exhibit, or is that hard to put into a museum exhibit?

Yes, there was something which I enjoyed doing very much because it helped bring the instruments to life, and that was we used sound. We had a series of about twelve recordings, each representing one or another of the instruments on display. And then we fixed it so that when a particular recording came on, a light flashed behind the instrument that was being represented, so that the audience didn't have to read any labels to see what instrument was being played: they could simply look and listen and enjoy the exhibit.

I wish I had seen that. You are not an American, are you, Mr. Turnbull?

No, I'm Scottish, but I probably shall be an American in a few years.

Where did you study anthropology?

At Oxford, in England.

JUNIUS B. BIRD

December 5, 1961

It is often hard to find Dr. Bird. His office is on the fifth floor, but he also has a large circular workroom in the sixth-floor tower where carefully mounted pieces of old fabric are examined under a big microscope. I finally caught up with him on the stairs, going from one room to the other, and sidetracked him into a temporarily empty office.

What are you doing right now, Dr. Bird?

Well, I'm going from this chair into another room where I am preparing material to go down to the IBM Service Bureau where they process coded data by machine.

The Service Bureau on Madison Avenue?

Yes. There's a whole lot of data we've accumulated in analyzing fabrics, archeological fabrics, some going back four thousand or more years.

What do you mean by fabrics?

Anything that's woven or twined, knotted, knitted, or otherwise created of yarn and fibers is a fabric. A piece of felt is a fabric. There are all sorts of ways of making fabric.

But among people who do not have machine looms, who do not have paper and pencil to plan what they intend to do, the creation of a fabric is a mental exercise, particularly when it comes to design. The woman who has no pencil or paper can't work out what she's going to do, as we might. She has to start out with a bit of yarn, and she has to start at the correct point, and she has to build it up.

There's an analogy with an image on a television tube. The image is produced by a series of little lines as the light travels back and forth, where the speed with which it travels is so great that our eyes cannot follow it, but it is built up row by row—one place it's light and one place it's dark—and it keeps on doing this so rapidly that it creates what seems to be a continuous solid image.

The same thing is true of structural design in a fabric. The figure or design starts at one point, as they put in the weft yarn, and the design is created row by row.

We have one nice example downstairs on exhibition at this moment in a special show, a piece of twining which is at least thirty-five hundred years old. The woman, or whoever made it, started out to create a complex figure. It is like an angular snake with a head on either end, and at the angles on either side there are rock crabs appended. She had to decide, in a space of about seven inches, where she should start the apex of one of the angles at the bottom of the space to be occupied by the figure. She miscalculated by about one quarter of an inch, an error which did not affect the total figure until after the first crab was nearly complete. By that time she realized that she was one quarter-inch too far to the right, so that when she came to the second crab, she did not have room to put in the four legs except by having them so thin that they wouldn't look right. So she compromised with nature and put in only three legs.

In that one little design, one figure of which is perhaps eleven and a half inches long by seven inches wide, there were over five thousand separate movements of the warp yarn, finger-manipulated, in the figure and about eight thousand more to create the background.

Is that fabric down in the special show on Peruvian art?

Yes, the old Peruvian materials that are exhibited on our first floor.

Well, I still don't see . . . Is it because of the analogy to television that you're going to IBM?

No, no. It's because in that piece, for instance, there's not only the design—which had a continuous record of use from the third millennium B.C. right to the time of the Spanish Conquest in the sixteenth century —in that piece, aside from the figure, there are warp yarns and there are weft yarns, all two-ply yarns. It happens that in that case they are entirely of cotton. But you also find yarn in which cotton and a plant fiber, a type of bast fiber, are blended or combined. If they blend the bast with cotton, they will use the blend in only one-half of the yarn. One ply will be cotton and bast, blended together, and the other ply will be pure cotton, the two twisted together. In setting up the warp they pair two yarns together; one will be pure cotton and one will be mixed, so that you have, in a working warp unit, about twenty-five per cent blended bast. And that's only one way in which the fibers are used. They will vary the twist direction of the yarn. I don't understand why they did that.

Dr. Bird, what are you going to give the IBM people?

Well, we have analyzed thousands of these old fabrics for the technical features of construction, for the yarn twists, for the fiber used, for the way the ends are finished, for the way the sides are finished, for their chronological position in the ground where they were excavated.

The objective is not just an analysis of textiles, but an analysis of textiles in relation to time. We want to see which features were constant throughout long centuries of use of certain techniques, certain materials. We do know that there were changes, that in certain periods there was an emphasis on the use of tapestry and at other times an emphasis on the use of embroidery or a multitude of different techniques.

And we plot all of these things against the archeological records—that is, where they were found in the ground, the sites they came from, the relationship of one type to another, one valley to another, all down through the desert areas. It gives us a body of data against which we can place unknowns, and it will show which features are constant and where there are alternative ways of doing the same thing, which ones were preferred.

Is this something you couldn't have done before computers? How many hundreds of years would it have taken?

It would take a long time to work it all out just by plotting it by hand, but it could be done. In fact, we are combining the use of a machine analyzer with a manual analysis of those features which are so rare that there is no point in processing them by machine. It has to be a combination. That is my specific job today.

Now, what is the most exciting thing you ever did in the past?

That's a very difficult question. People think that archeology is something that has highlights all the time or at least occasionally. Something like finding King Tut's tomb. Granted that that was probably the highlight in the professional life of the man who discovered it; but undoubtedly the biggest pleasure comes from rounding out our knowledge of the past and filling in gaps. And that is true in my own work. I have occasionally found things which were rare or unusual, and they do give you a little excitement at the time, like finding treasure perhaps. But the real satisfaction comes from assembling all of your data, recreating a picture of past life. So as I say, it is difficult to point to any one thing, any one moment.

Perhaps, if you want a specific example . . . I spent the first two-and-a-half years after I was married in southern Chile. We made a survey of a region measuring about a thousand miles north to south, part of it an island archipelago where the weather is terrible. We had our own little boat and followed the coast searching for archeological material.

Did your wife go with you?

Oh, yes, in spite of the fact that she'd never camped out before or done anything like that.

How old were you?

I suppose about twenty-seven.

Was that your first field trip, when you were twenty-seven?

No, but I'm leading up to just one little point, which was exciting at the time. As I say, we spent about two-and-a-half years in the region and felt that we had recovered enough information so that we had good continuity for the human occupation of that area for thousands of years, going back to the time when one of the glacial lakes of that area was at a much higher level than it is today and received water from the melting ice.

We thought we had finished with the southern area and were headed back north, as winter was coming on, when we heard of a little cave in a volcanic crater about one hundred and fifty miles from the nearest town, out in the grassland area. Everybody warned us that if we went there and it came on to snow, we'd have to abandon our truck and walk out.

The cave was close to the Argentine border and had

been used by smugglers. As caves go, it was a beauty. You could walk inside—in fact, you could ride in on horseback, the mouth was high enough—and it was about forty feet deep, so you could get well out of the wind. This is a very windy area, and any campsite there is better if it is protected from the wind, naturally. The floor in this one was level, and was dusty from the campfires left by the shepherds and smugglers who had used it last. In cleaning out the recent debris, out came a little tin can; it rolled into the light with the label still legible on it, a label saying this was a can of Brun's butter. Brun was a packer of butter in Denmark, and about four years before, I had worked in northeast Greenland where Hans, his son, had worked with me. So here at the Strait of Magellan was a tin of Brun's butter as the first find in this particular cave.

Well, we went to it, and as we continued to excavate we found the record we were already familiar with from checking some hundreds of other sites. Near the bottom we found evidence of a volcanic eruption, a volcanic ash layer. On the surface of the ash, at the rear of the cave, there were some blocks of stone. As I moved them, the bones of a large animal were exposed. We hadn't found bones of such size before, but knew there had been a type of large animal in the area a long time ago, an animal now extinct, known as the Mylodon, or ground sloth. As we brushed the dust from our finds, we recognized them as sloth bones, and with them were man-made flakes of stone, basalt.

No one had ever found such evidence of the coexistence of these extinct animals with human remains. Yet, here it was, and at the end of our season. Winter had started; we had been warned we couldn't stay there. One of the men on the sheep ranch had told us, "I've always suspected that cave has a passageway going back into the rocks, so if you don't have time to explore it, don't fill up the entrance. Leave it open and I'll go on back."

Well, there wasn't time for a dig to take these things out properly. I removed only a few to make photographs and drawings. Our friend had asked me to leave the entrance open. But if he discovered the bones and word got around, it would be all torn apart and the record would be spoiled. So I left a note saying he could see for himself that the cave did not continue.

To discourage further digging I heaped up the dirt at the visible end of the trench into a cone shaped like a huge ant lion trap. Ant lions are little creatures that eat other insects. Here in New York State you can find them in almost any dry spot under a rock ledge where there's powdery soil. In the larval state the ant lion lives in this dust. Then he flicks up the dirt with a movement of his tail and creates a little conical crater. He lives at the bottom, and if an ant or some other insect tries to cross the crater, it slips down the slope and can't climb out. As it sinks to the bottom the ant lion, lying in wait in the dust, seizes and devours it.

In the case of our cave, the dirt was a fine, dry, powdery dust, just right for faking an ant lion trap. So I heaped it high around the opening at the end of the trench, at the maximum angle of stability. One touch and it would start to slide down, exactly like a giant ant lion trap. The point was to discourage anyone from disturbing the area, and it worked. When we went back in the spring, the trench had not been disturbed, though, clearly, somebody had been down there.

Well, the point of all this is that the discovery and the recognition of those old bones and artifacts was exciting. But the real pleasure came from the final and complete excavation, and the establishment of what sort of implements the people had and what they themselves were like (we found their cremated bones in the same cave). Since then, the age of the oldest remains has been measured by carbon fourteen analysis as close to eleven thousand years.

Now, what do you want most to do next?

Well, there are so many things that are of interest and importance in South American archeology, which I'm most concerned with, that it's hard to define or pick out any one. I would like very much to work again in Peru and to concentrate not so much on the levels which yield textiles and the later levels which yield pottery and gold and more elaborate cultural material, but to search for the remains of the nomadic hunters, the people who were associated with extinct animals.

The last time I was down there I found a few fragmentary bones of an extinct mastodon exposed on workshop sites, associated with broken bones and stone implements. We can't say even that the creature was killed by these people, for these are wind-eroded sites. The stone artifacts might have been more recent, previously resting in soil above the level of the elephant remains. There is a chance that they were contemporary, but we need a better situation than the ones we discovered to establish the fact. I think a survey up and down the coastal areas would be well worth while and would produce results.

You want to go back in time to before those beautiful textiles and gold things shown down in the exhibit—you want to go way back in time now?

Yes, there must be human remains in Peru which are at least eleven thousand years old, and probably more.

There ought to be a great deal more, wouldn't you say?

There might be. There is some indication that there were people in the Americas between twenty and thirty thousand years ago. It is very unsatisfactory evidence; I don't deny that it is a possibility, but the evidence is not too convincing.

ROBERT L. CARNEIRO and GERTRUDE E. DOLE

October 10, 1961

This office, down a different corridor, is very crowded and very neat. Lying on the table are a number of specimens from the Indian tribes of the Amazon area. Dr. Carneiro's anthropologist wife, Dr. Gertrude Dole, is working with him today, and they both answer questions. Their initials (if not the comments themselves) will identify which of them is speaking as the conversation shifts.

Do you both work here?

(RC) I do, all the time, and Trudie does, part of the time.

(GD) And when I work here I work without pay, not officially.

And you use your own name for your anthropological work?

Yes.

And what were you doing just at this moment?

(RC) When you came in I had just finished a section on the next to the last chapter of the monograph that we're doing on the Kuikuru Indians of Central Brazil.

You've just finished?

Yes, the section on intertribal relations I had just concluded the minute you came in.

So you felt pretty good, I guess.

It's always nice to get a section out of the way.

Well, now, isn't this the place where you both went and worked?

That's right.

When did you go?

We were there in 1953–54.

Do you plan to go back?

No, we had plans to go back for the summer two years ago, but they fell through.

So you're just writing up your 1953–54 field trip?

That's right.

Did you do any collecting on the field trip?

Yes, we made a collection of some one hundred and fifty specimens, most of which are here in the Museum now.

(GD) These specimens were divided among three museums. We left some in the National Museum in Rio de Janeiro, we left others in the Museum of Anthropology at the University of Michigan, and brought the rest here.

Was Michigan where you did your graduate work?

Yes, both of us.

Were you going to be an anthropologist before you met your husband?

Yes, before my husband had decided to go into anthropology, as a matter of fact.

Did you convert him?

I think not; it was sort of a parallel evolution.

Now, what was the most exciting thing that you found in your fieldwork?

(RC) Exciting, in a scientific way, was discovering that a village that lived under "slash-and-burn" cultivation could remain permanently settled.

What does "slash-and-burn" mean?

Slash-and-burn is a technique of farming in which you first cut over a section of forest and let the vegetation lie drying during the dry season, and just before the rains you burn it—burn as much of it as you can—and then plant between the logs and the stumps. You do this for two or three years and then abandon the plot and clear another one. Well, it's ordinarily thought that people who live this way can't have permanent villages. But the Kuikuru have been in the same locale for about ninety years without having to move.

(GD) When they do move, their reasons are not horticultural. They once moved because of trouble with relatives and split to form a new village. The reasons they move their houses within the area which they now occupy are usually supernatural. They fear their location is not favorable because they've had some disease or they find too many burials in the plot where they've made graves. Or, on one occasion, they found that water from the lake was rising and entering the graves.

Are you specially interested in horticulture?

(RC) Yes, that's one of my main interests in ethnology.

How about you?

(GD) I'm particularly interested in the social organization. I'm interested also in the fact that the nine tribes in the region we studied are culturally almost identical although they represent tribes from four different language groups. They have acculturated one another to the extent that now one can scarcely tell one tribe from another except by their language. They all have practically the same social organization, which couldn't have been the case originally.

Do you know which one started it?

Yes. We know that the tribes which represent the Arawak and Carib groups were the earliest in the area, and that the Tupian tribes came in quite recently. But the most recent one is the Trumai tribe, which has no close language affiliations with any other group in the tropical forest, so far as we know.

Were these Caribs the Indians that the Caribbean was named after?

That's right, they're of the same language family, and it seems they must have migrated thirteen hundred miles up the Xingú River from the center of Carib development on the Caribbean coast, probably in the Orinoco area.

Do you have any idea how long ago?

They seem to have arrived in the upper Xingú region only a few hundred years ago.

Is there any archeology for these people? Has anyone worked on this?

(RC) Yes, we did some digging in that area. No professional archeologist has worked there yet. There's a great deal to be done.

You must have had to do almost everything then yourselves. Isn't that so?

Yes, we were there, just the two of us, with one hundred forty-five Kuikuru.

(GD) And we didn't have them cook for us or do other services, except very incidental ones.

You did all that yourself, too. And photography—did you take any movies?

Yes.

And you had to do your own digging, too. Did you do any measurements, any physical anthropology?

(RC) No, that we didn't do. Some of that had been done. In fact, the earliest ethnologists to go into the area were some Germans who went in the early 1880's and '90's. They did a certain amount of anthropometry, and we just didn't think we should take the time to do it.

Did you learn the language?

To a certain extent we did.

(GD) We used the native language almost exclusively, because there were only two persons among the Kuikuru who could speak Portuguese.

And Portuguese would have been the intermediary language. Did you speak it?

(RC) Yes, well enough to use it. One of the two Portuguese speakers was a very unreliable person and we didn't want to use him more than we needed to absolutely. The other man was a very hard worker and was generally away from the village. So we had to fall back on Kuikuru and learn as much as we could and as soon as we could.

Did you use these two Portuguese speakers as interpreters while you were learning the language?

Yes.

Now, what are you hoping to do next?

(GD) Well, we've already got another batch of field notes from the Peruvian Montaña that we'll have to write up.

This was another trip?

Last year, 1960–61.

How long were you there?

We were among the Indians about six months.

And were these very different Indians?

Yes, they belong to the general tropical-forest horticultural type, but their language is quite separate, their gardening is less advanced, and they depend on hunting much more.

What do they hunt?

They hunt tapir, deer, peccaries, monkeys, birds, rodents of various types.

Did they have less permanent villages, too?

(RC) Yes. As a matter of fact, that's one of the interesting features of their settlement pattern. They often live in single family houses scattered around, and the nearest thing to a village will be several houses, each a couple of hundred yards away from the other, so they have nothing like the relatively large and tidy villages of the upper Xingú area, where the houses are all close together.

Did you have to follow them around on their hunting trips?

Well, I went on one hunting trip with them. It's not easy to do. They proceed very rapidly, and we were in a position where we couldn't follow them very often or very far.

(GD) But we did go fishing with them, to see them catch fish with bow and arrow and also with poison.

But you could establish a spot where you could see enough of them, where they camped?

Yes. We saw a lot of them; we saw a lot of their culture.

Now, did they live scattered all over the place?

They traditionally—in the last few decades at any rate—they have lived in small groups, such as an extended family, each family on a separate stream. But they are in communication with each other. Now, the place we studied is becoming a more nucleated group because people have come from various streams and settled near a mission. But they still build their houses several hundred yards apart and out of sight, so they can't communicate except by hollering and that isn't very effective.

Do they have a hollering kind of language? Shouting from one spot to another?

(RC) Yes. For example, if a man comes home and he's bagged a tapir, which is an animal much too large to carry home by himself, he might cut off a part of it and bring it back and then holler to the other men and ask them, in a sort of shorthand way, if they will come with him the next day, in the morning, to go out and finish cutting up the animal. Whatever part each man brings home is his.

(GD) This communication isn't usually complete unless it's prearranged, because their standardized signals are so few. For example, someone may shout, "Ho, come eat!" or "Ho, come carry tapir," and so forth, while the other calls back, "Ho, I'm coming," or some such common answer.

WALTER A. FAIRSERVIS, JR.

October 18, 1961

Dr. Walter Fairservis does not work in an office. Instead, he works at a crowded table in a room jammed with cupboards and bookcases and tables on which objects are spread out. There are even a large number of brightly colored things hanging from the ceiling, done up in cellophane. He is a very tall man and wears a brown smock. When he stands up, his head seems lost among the bright hanging packages.

What are you doing this minute?

I'm working on prehistoric man. As you know, archeology is one part of anthropology. It has to do with man's life in the past. And as an archeologist I'm interested in trying to revive ancient cultures, so we'll have some understanding of just why man does certain things in the present, by getting a view of his past—of the origins of the various things that are important in everyday life.

Well, what are you doing this afternoon, this minute, in this room?

At this minute I'm working on civilization—on a paper which is to come out telling something about our present knowledge of what civilization really is, as it is expressed in the very early civilizations.

Would all those things up there in cellophane have anything to do with your present paper?

No. Those are Chinese things. Actually, I'm doing some work on the beginnings of Chinese civilization, but these are kites that come from late nineteenth-century China. They have to do with the old way of life. These kites were flown at particular festival occasions, and we're cataloguing them and cleaning them. Students of this kind of thing can learn a great deal about Chinese festivals, and certain things about their religion and about their entertainments, and so on, as they are expressed on these rather fancy kites.

Did you ever work in China?

I've been in China. I've never done any ethnology in China, but I've been on a number of archeological sites in China and seen something of early Chinese culture.

What's the most exciting thing that you've done in the last couple of years?

Well, the most exciting thing, I suppose, is going out into the field in Pakistan, which is the place that I'm particularly interested in, and finding indications of early civilization out there.

Did you make any very exciting finds?

It all depends on what you call exciting. Actually, on this last trip, we went to a place on the borders of India and Pakistan, where we found ruins that were almost like Pompeii in their preservation—beautifully preserved, and they date much before Pompeii, they date around two thousand years before Christ. There was a whole village of ancient times, and you can actually walk up and down the streets and see something of the layout of houses and find things that relate to their everyday life.

When you say "found," what does that mean?

As you know, archeology is a science, and when we go into the field we go out with a specific problem in mind and a specific area to work in, and when we find these things they are the result of a systematic survey in which we go over a certain geographic area looking for evidence of ancient man.

But nobody knew that this city was there?

No, this was just one of those fortunate accidents. We knew that there were things there, but we didn't know that they would be in such excellent preservation.

Then the first part is science, and only later you look to see whether the things are well preserved?

And that's sheer good fortune, yes.

What are you going to do next?

Well, I hope I can get back out there and carry on some excavations and explore a little further to see if we can't learn more about what life was like on the borders of India, two thousand years before Christ.

You want to go back to the place where you were?

Yes, where we were surveying.

Is that what you're going to do next?

Well, I'm planning to; it depends again on the most practical side of the field, and that's money.

What are you going to do in the next two or three months?

I've been invited by the government of India to go over for the hundredth anniversary of the founding of their department of archeology. There's going to be a big meeting there and also the opening of their national museum. I'm going over there as a guest of the government of India, to give a lecture and to meet other archeologists and to get some ideas of what India is doing in its archeology.

Did you say this was the hundredth anniversary of an Indian university's department of archeology?

No. The Archaeological Survey of India was founded in 1861 by Sir Alexander Cunningham, when the British were in control. The Survey is under the government. It was always under the government, under British control, and it's still under the government in the present day.

So they've been studying archeology for a hundred years over there too?

Yes. Of course, the British were the ones who originally got them going in it. Now they have their own archeological school, and they're actually training students from other countries in their school—it's one of the best in the world.

From which other countries?

Burma sent some; Ceylon and Iran—among those that I know.

Could Americans go there?

Oh, yes, by all means. In fact, as I understand it, there are some Europeans there, but I haven't met them.

The teaching is in English, is it?

Yes. In fact, the older teachers were trained at Oxford, Cambridge, and London. And Sir Mortimer Wheeler, who was the Director of Archeology for India for years, had a training school right in India, and many of the Indian archeologists are graduates of it. It's very, very good.

Have you done any other very exciting fieldwork?

Well, we were the first archeological expedition

from the United States to work in Afghanistan, and we did find the first remnants there of prehistoric man in Afghanistan, right after the war. Afghanistan is a very important link between East and West in Asia, and it's very exciting because it has representations of many, many cultures, both of the present and of ancient times.

And you didn't have any difficulty working in Afghanistan? Were the people friendly?

The people were perfectly friendly. I think our greatest difficulty was the fact that when we first went there, it was rather primitive and we had to bring everything we needed with us. When our cars broke down and our food went low, we did have some strain. But that's all part of it.

GORDON F. EKHOLM

December 5, 1961

The sign on Dr. Gordon Ekholm's door reads, "Curator of Mexican Archeology." But the door is hard to find because it is set deep between huge banks of storage cabinets. On top of these are several large stone-like casts. One of these is a corn god, the original of which once decorated a Mayan temple in Honduras; another, a different version of the corn deity, is a goddess, an Aztec piece from Veracruz. There is also a huge burial urn from western Mexico and a fierce, magnificent stylized jaguar whose sloping back forms a *metate*—a stone for grinding corn.

What are you doing at this moment?

I'm writing a letter to a person in South America, a director of an anthropological institute down there. He wants me to do an article for him on something I'm very interested in—the question of wheeled toys in America and their possible meaning in regard to diffusion from the Old World to the New World. This seems to be an awfully exciting thing to many people.

Why is it exciting?

Well, because it's off the beaten track in anthropology. It's a little bit against the usual assumption about the origin of the American Indian cultures.

Is it the wheel itself that is the point?

No, it's the fact that previously we always thought that in America there were no wheels. But we can actually prove that there were wheels, and the problem is, how the invention occurred.

But they're only found on toys?

Let's say they are only found on little objects.

Dr. Ekholm, what are your special areas of work as an archeologist?

My interest is in Mexico and Central America.

The whole of Mexico and Central America?

Yes. That includes the Aztecs and the Maya and many other less well-known peoples.

What's the most exciting thing you've done within the last two or three years?

I think perhaps the most exciting thing was working in a Mayan site down in southern Mexico in the State of Tabasco, where we ran a couple of expeditions. It was a large ceremonial site—something I'd never worked in before.

There were large buildings, and they were all constructed of brick. Practically all other Mayan cities are of stone; this was a very unusual one, built of brick. Of course, they look like other Maya buildings, but the use of brick raises other questions, such as the origin of the whole technique of using this material.

Now, this brick building—was it older or younger than the other ones?

About the same age as the other type of Maya work.

Where do you think the brick came from?

I don't know. It's probably an invention coming from the very region. The lowlands on the east coast—the particular region of this site—is an alluvial plain where there is no stone, and supposedly they wanted to build and had no material and invented the use of fired brick. This is similar to other parts of the world where the need for a material has probably caused an invention.

And are they exactly the same kind of bricks that are found in other parts of the world?

Oh, no. They're quite different. They were not made in molds. They were cut out of big slabs of wet clay put on the ground, probably with a big knife. They're not all the same size, like our bricks.

So it really is probably a separate invention?

It probably is.

And what is the thing you want to do next?

I don't know precisely. I'm getting more interested, perhaps, than I used to be, in the study of the art of Middle America. And I want to do more general studies on the art of certain areas, such as the Huasteca, which is a little section in northern Mexico. A great deal of stone sculpture comes from there. No one has ever studied it, and I want to do something with that.

Would this be from the standpoint of an art critic, that you'd be looking at it?

No, it would be from the standpoint of an anthropologist; I would look to see where it originated, what relationships it had with Mayan sculpture and the art from other portions of Mexico.

Do you care whether it's beautiful or not?

Yes, very much; I care very much. That's what brings me to have some interest in it. The Huasteca is where I worked for some years on general archeological problems, where I made excavations and established a chronology. I want to set up a chronology for the sculpture to see the history of the art and as evidence for other things.

You do a lot of collecting for the Museum?

A fair amount of collecting for the Museum, yes.

Have you got a hall of your own?

Yes, I have a hall, the Mexican Hall, on the second floor. We have a very fine collection there of things from Mexico and from the Maya area.

Have you any children, Dr. Ekholm?

Yes, I have two children. One of them is becoming an archeologist.

Oh? That's what I was going to ask you. Did you ever take them along anywhere?

Not into the field. Mainly because we go into the field in Mexico usually in the wintertime, and it's always a question of getting away from school. If we had only one, perhaps, it would have been easier, but with one child younger, it's too difficult to take them into the field. But my daughter is now studying anthropology and went into the field last summer in Ecuador.

Where is she studying anthropology?

She's at Radcliffe. She's a junior this year and enjoying it a great deal.

And she got a chance to go into the field when she was a sophomore?

Yes, when she was a sophomore, which is something new in anthropology study. She went with a Columbia University group, with Dr. Harris in charge, to Ecuador.

Do you think more students are going to get a chance to go into the field earlier?

Yes, definitely.

STANLEY A. FREED

October 18, 1961

Compared with the other offices, Dr. Freed's looks as if he is camping out. His desk is in one corner of a big empty room. It is, in fact, part of the old library quarters (the library has been moved to the fourth floor), and the rooms are to be made over into storerooms.

Meanwhile, until an office can be arranged for him, Dr. Freed, one of the youngest of the curators, just camps. A couple of bookcases are pushed against the wall, and on the floor, spread out on sheets of brown paper, are a lot of small tools, arranged as they later will be in a museum case down in the Hall of the Indians of the Northwest Coast. Some pictures of North American Indian house types are on the table.

Dr. Freed, what are you curator of, here?

I'm curator of North American ethnology.

That means you know about Indians. Did you do any fieldwork among Indians?

Yes, I did it with two tribes.

Which ones?

I visited the Washo in western Nevada and eastern California for about six months, and then I briefly visited the Mohave in southern California, for only a few weeks.

Is that your whole fieldwork—are you only interested in American Indians?

No, I'm interested also in the people of India, and I spent twenty-one months there doing fieldwork.

Which was the more interesting, the North American Indians or the people of India?

Oh, you really can't say. I would say they were equally interesting. They were very different. And the fact that I was able to visit groups as different as these were, I think gave me a much better insight into people in general.

Were the people in India primitive?

Absolutely not. Extremely sophisticated. You couldn't call them primitive.

But you do call it fieldwork?

Certainly.

Was there any difference in the way you worked? When you worked in India, did you still work by listening to what people said, mainly, or did you use other methods?

Well, yes, there was a considerable difference in the way I worked. With North American Indians, at least in the type of study I was doing among them, I was trying to get the aboriginal culture, or as much of it as was left. And this meant long interviews with elderly people, whereas in India I was interested in what was going on right then, at that particular time. Consequently I depended a great deal more in India on observation than on interviewing.

Did you go alone?

My wife was with me. She's an anthropologist, too.

Where did you meet her?

In graduate school.

She already knew she was going to be an anthropologist?

Yes, before she met me; she was already studying anthropology in graduate school.

And you worked together in the field?

Absolutely.

How old are you, Dr. Freed?

I'm thirty-four.

And you've had three trips, is that right?

Yes, three trips.

And what are you doing right this minute, this morning?

I just finished writing a preface to a book, and now that I've finished that I'm going to start writing some labels for some exhibits, and . . .

Whose book?

The book is Kluckhohn and Leighton's *The Navaho*. It's being reissued in our soft-cover series, and the curators are doing the prefaces.

When I came in you were telephoning about something.

I was telephoning about the preface, yes.

And then you were going to start writing labels?

I'm going to start working on labels for a new Northwest Coast Indians hall we just installed.

What does writing labels mean? What do you have to do?

Well, in this case I am faced with an exhibit already established, so I don't have to plan the story that is going to be told in the case; that's already been given to me. What I have to do is look at the case, figure out what story is there, and then try to write a label which will guide people when they're viewing the case and make it more meaningful to them.

You mean, in other words, that great big hall full of totem poles on the first floor of the Museum. Which case are you going to write labels for this morning?

I'm working on the Tlingit alcove, and the case that I'm going to be working on right away is the armor these people wore—wooden slat armor or rawhide armor of various kinds. It's a Siberian trait, really, or it's assumed to be, and I'm going to write a label about warfare, armor, and weapons of war, and things like that.

Now that's an old, old hall, isn't it?

Yes, I don't know exactly, but I think it went up about 1900—between then and 1910. The collecting was done mainly in the 1890's. That was when most of the Jesup North Pacific expeditions were in the field.

And most of the people that went on those expeditions are dead, aren't they?

They are, yes.

Well, when you want to make a new label, what do you use?

It's extremely interesting. We have the old labels, we have the catalogues, and we have the published material. Now the old labels, I think, contain material that's neither in the catalogues nor in the books and monographs. The second thing is, there have been things published since that work was done, which in many ways are more authoritative. The recent people who wrote them had more to go on. Sometimes what's in the new books conflicts with what's on the labels, and then one's faced, of course, with making a decision. I'm inclined to think the new stuff is more trustworthy.

You really have to know everything. . . .

Absolutely. You have to go to the catalogues, you have to review the labels, and you have to look at all the pertinent literature—at least at the major things and the major sources, and read it all and understand it. And then once you've digested it all, then you sit down and present your two hundred or one hundred words or whatever it is, concisely stating what it's about.

You have to know who wrote that old label?

It would help, it would really help if I did know, but I don't know.

That's one big problem, then, to know whether it's accurate or not?

Yes, that's a big problem. I found a lot of mistakes; at least, I think they're mistakes.

To guess who wrote some of those labels you have to know the history of the Museum as well, don't you?

That helps too, yes.

Can you find it out?

You get it by osmosis.

What's the next thing you're going to do?

Let me see. The next thing I'm going to do after the labels, and the labels is a job that's going to continue for weeks. . . .

I don't mean today, but what's the next exciting thing in the world you're going to do?

To me, the next exciting thing in the world will be writing a monograph on part of the research I did in India. Heaven knows how long it will take, but with luck I should have it fairly well in hand by this summer. And then, following that, I would like to think about a field trip among the North American Indians.

You're the North American Indian curator, here at the Museum, and yet in the immediate future you'll be writing about India. Isn't this a conflict?

Well, there's an overriding principle involved here. We're all anthropologists, and if you're writing about anthropology, that covers a lot of ground.

You're not pinned down to one area, then?

No. You have a great deal of freedom.

JOAN P. MENCHER

October 18, 1961

Next to Dr. Freed's office is another barnlike room, still filled with library shelves. Sitting at a table close to the wall is a very pretty girl who does not look old enough to have earned the Ph.D. that follows her name on the door. But she has already made her first field trip to India. She has a New York accent that is a little softened by a touch of another language, as if she changed her way of speaking while she was in India and has not quite changed back. On the table are some very old books opened at old-fashioned drawings.

What were you working on right this minute as I walked in the door?

Well, as you walked in through the door, I was going through some rather old books, looking for descriptions of traditional house types and settlement patterns in various parts of India. That is in connection with a small part of what I'm doing this year as a Fellow in the Museum of Natural History.

Are you doing this for the Museum? That is, is it something connected with an exhibit here?

No, this is my own research. Right now, I am doing reading and looking up material on the distribution of certain items of culture in India, in connection with one piece of research that I'm working on now, namely, the distribution of house types and settlement patterns.

Is this something you're doing out of a book?

What I'm doing is using any material that I know from the field and trying to get information from books and from anthropologists who have worked in India. This is really just the beginning of a piece of research. I am also making use of what I know from the area where I worked and any place that I visited.

You went to India?

That's right. I went to India in 1958, right after I got my doctorate from Columbia University.

How did you get there?

I went on a combination of two fellowships. One was from the American Association of University Women and the other was a Fulbright travel grant.

How long was it possible to stay on your grants?

I was in India about twenty-one months, but because of various things connected with the Fulbright grant, I was in Kerala only the last sixteen months.

Did you learn the language?

I got so I could understand it. I can't speak it too fluently. I had a woman interpreter. One of the difficulties with speaking the language was that I couldn't start to study it in America because at that time there weren't any grammar books or dictionaries available for my personal use.

What is the language?

The language is spoken by a small number of people in the State of Kerala—actually, about sixteen million, but that is small compared to India's population. It's called Malayalam. It's a very complex and intricate kind of language with a complex grammar, complex sound structure, and so on. For example, there are three "r"-like sounds that my tongue and ear still have difficulty distinguishing. This is more than I found in any other major Indian language.

But you worked on it after you got there?

Yes. Actually, today it is taught at the University of Pennsylvania.

You went all by yourself?

That's right.

Did you have any problems as a woman going all alone?

No. I can't say that one wouldn't in any part of the world, but where I was, I was always considered as one of the females of the family or the group, and people were very understanding, protective, and helpful.

Were there things you couldn't find out, things you couldn't work on, because you are a woman?

To some extent. I had a feeling that there were certain types of information that I lacked. I couldn't for example, go and stay in certain of the coffee shops where only men went and especially where men might drink. On the other hand, there were things that I could do that no male anthropologist could do in the field. There's material I got from the women, and there were places where I was allowed to be with women where no man would ever have been permitted, because it is against the local customs and ideas.

What kinds of places?

The kitchen. No man, especially a strange man, would have been allowed in there. Or in the female quarters of the house, where no man except a husband would be permitted.

What did you do when you first came back from the field?

When I first came back from the field I taught for a year in one of the colleges in a suburb of New York. I was teaching a combination of anthropology and some sociology.

And then?

Then I received a fellowship from the Museum for this year, which is enabling me to analyze and write up much of my material from Malabar, as well as start work on this study of house types and settlement patterns.

And what are you going to do next?

I'm not certain. I'd like to do more research, preferably. I'd like to combine it with teaching, but I'd like to teach something related to my own field of interest.

Where do you want to go next?

I would like to do more work in South Asia anyway, preferably in India. I feel that it is such a large country with such a vast tradition, and with so much to learn one can't really do enough in one field trip.

PHILIP C. GIFFORD

December 5, 1961

Mr. Gifford also is hard to find. His office is a busy place, but he seems to be everywhere at once—up in the storerooms; talking to a Customs official about clearing a new collection; arranging to get out a loan exhibit that will travel a circuit of museums; talking with an old lady who has brought in two carvings from her attic. And when he isn't in any of these places, he is "down in the Hall."

"Down in the Hall" is on the fourth floor, directly under the Anthropology Department offices, but it is necessary to walk a long distance to get there. From the elevator you walk through the Age of Man Hall, lined with huge, tusked mammoths, snarling saber-toothed tigers, and other animals that were living when man first appeared. Ahead, over the inner doorway, is an enormous painting of a group of cavemen huddled around a freshly killed deer. Looking up, you can read its title, "Men of the Early New Stone Age After a Stag Hunt in Northern France." Just beyond, protected by heavy iron gates, is the Morgan Hall of Gems, with its cases filled with great lumps of precious minerals—a hall that girl students never want to leave.

Finally, there is the heavy iron gate at the other end and a big sign, "Not Open to the Public." Beyond this gate, at last, is "the Hall." In it are many tall old cases stacked full of spears, arrows, and masks, and down its length trestle tables are set up with orderly rows of objects spread on them and open catalogue books. Standing in the doorway, you can look through to the far end where a great Easter Island statue stands.

In the center, also on a trestle table, is a miniature model of what this hall—"the new hall"—will look like when the preparations are complete. Looking into the model, you can see the tiny cases made of cellophane, each of which has miniature color photographs of the specimens arranged inside. This new method of designing a hall was invented by the designer in charge, Preston McClanahan. As the specimens were selected for each case, they were spread out and photographed in color for cutouts, like paper dolls, so that the specimens themselves would not have to be handled over and over again and could be put away.

And here in the hall, I catch up with Philip Gifford.

Mr. Gifford, you have a lot of stuff down here, it seems to me. What are you doing? Is this a workshop?

This is a combination of storage and laboratory, with

some housekeeping going on at the same time. It all sort of flows together. What we're eventually attempting to do down here is to consolidate all the collections of materials from two halls and organize them into distinct groups—those chosen for the new exhibition and those to be returned to storage.

What was this hall before, where we are right now?

This is Section Six, and had been called the Pacific Island Hall. Now this one and the hall next to it, Section Eight, are to be condensed. Section Eight had been the Philippine Islands Hall, and now both these halls will be combined into one Hall of the Peoples of the Pacific. Material from both halls and related pieces from the storerooms will be coordinated here and sorted out. This means actually stripping the Philippine and Pacific Island storerooms to the bare walls to allow us to select the new exhibits from a complete range of specimens.

Now, when you say it's a laboratory, what do you mean exactly?

During the early days of the Museum there were very unsystematic attempts at cataloguing. Some of the pieces have an importance that goes far beyond their history as given in the catalogue, and looking at such pieces now, with our present resources and publications, we can reassess their value in relation to early cultures. This is the process I'm going to carry on, as well as adding information on the pieces for the catalogue.

Give me an example. What's that bowl over there? The black one with something like mother-of-pearl on it and a rooster's head?

This is one of our problems. It's a piece that came in early in the Museum's history and was collected by a man who, as far as I know, has been quite reliable in all the pieces he's brought in. The bowl itself is from the Solomon Islands, and it's quite characteristic, but it has a separate piece of carving—done in a style that is typical of the northern part of New Ireland—joined to it with metal pins. The two places have distinct art styles, and this bowl is made up of one part from each. It's an unusual thing. The question now is how it got into its present state, because it was never used this way by the natives.

When I came in the other day, I saw you through an open door up on the fifth floor and you had a big collection of things spread out there, some big wooden things—the John Brandt collection. What is that?

This is a collection that was offered to the Museum for possible purchase and we have it on loan here now. It was being assessed for the value of the collection as it applies to our needs and desires here. Several of the curators have looked at it, and the idea now is to try to figure out which pieces we can use or whether we should like to hold on to all the pieces and use them for study and exhibition.

Did you find out anything new from that collection?

Well, this collection is interesting because it has a

lot of very modern carvings that are alike, but different from earlier carvings from the same islands. These pieces were systematically collected, but they were collected at a later date from the collections that we do have at the Museum. And the difference in style is quite interesting, actually.

You have to have a very good memory, don't you, Mr. Gifford, to remember all these different styles when you're working with them? Do you like working with so many different kinds of things?

I seem to be able to remember pieces better than numbers or biographical records. One of my hopes is that sooner or later, after I get the collections fairly well memorized, I will be able to do some sort of synthesis of the art styles.

Are you particularly interested in the art styles of any one society?

Why, I recently started working with the New Ireland material we have here, because New Ireland is an area that is secluded. It hasn't been exposed to a great deal of influence—or hadn't been at the time our collections were made—from other cultures. And my studies on the New Ireland art have been aimed primarily at trying to discover whether there is any kind of symbolism that can be traced in these pieces, and how this symbolism can be related to the early culture of New Ireland. This is a difficult job because there isn't a great deal of history, really good ethnological observation, with regard to the early culture. And I'm wondering if it may not be possible to predicate something of the culture from the art styles. This is a kind of tricky process, and it needs very careful work.

And you keep on working with the— Oh, I see, that's what you mean by New Ireland art. Do you work with each of these big heads separately, as they are spread out on the table? Or how are you going to handle them when you start working on the style?

There are different art styles within the New Ireland area. Different parts of the island produce different types of material, and these can be grouped. And we also try to find what we can that has been accurately dated and positioned on New Ireland.

How do you find that out?

Through the Museum record. When material is first brought into the Museum, whatever information we have as to its collection or importance or use is put down in the records.

Then will you get at what's here in this collection? Or do other museums have things from New Ireland that you'd have to look at, too?

Well, other museums have collections, and some are much larger than the one we have. Our collection happens to be one that has not been studied up to this point, and I feel that if I can become thoroughly aware of all the intricate details of this one collection, then

I'll be better prepared to go off and look at the others and compare them with ours.

So you will someday go and look at collections in other places. Where?

There are several very good collections. One is at Chicago, and there are some collections in Europe, in the German and the Swiss museums, that are very old and quite good. There is also a large collection in Sydney, Australia. The point about New Ireland is that, as of now, the natives are no longer making any carvings of this type, and all of the art symbolism that I'm interested in will have to be more or less deduced from the pieces that were made in the past.

If a young anthropologist went out there now, would he find anybody making any of these things?

An anthropologist who went out in 1957 to one island off the coast of New Ireland found that they still were making what they called *malagan* figures, but these are a far cry from what the early pieces were. They're crude and they have many features which make them unmistakably modern. And the question is how long even these pieces will be manufactured. Because *malagan* has to do with the religious side of native life, and when missionary influence has changed the whole basis of life then the carving will disappear. It has already in most parts of New Ireland, and there is only one little section left.

So you're really working right here in the Museum with a vanished civilization?

That's what it amounts to, I think.

And is working on the art styles of the Pacific the thing you're most interested in doing next?

I think the New Ireland problem is one that can be looked at more or less as one whole problem—you don't have to look for influences from all over Polynesia or China or for transpacific contact or anything like that. But once a methodology has been arrived at in evaluating the importance of the various elements of style in the New Ireland culture, this technique might be applied, possibly with modifications, to other parts of the Pacific.

So you're going to do your scientific work right here in the Museum or in other museums or out of books, because the things you're working with you can't even dig up any more. Is that right?

I'm afraid that's probably true, yes.

That's the difference between you and an archeologist, isn't it? Archeologists have to go and dig things up from the ground, and you have to dig them up in the Museum.

Everything that comes in has to be interpreted. The archeologist tries to interpret his material through looking at the ethnological part, and then, too, there are ethnologists who work on material things which are no longer being made, so they have to look back in the old ethnology, in the old books primarily.

Books in other languages?

And books in other languages, yes.

In how many other languages are the books you want to find things in?

Some places in the Pacific have changed hands several times, and the people who have been responsible for New Ireland have written in German and in French, besides English. They don't speak any Dutch in New Ireland.

What kind of techniques do you have for the physical side of your kind of work? Do you have to know how to protect all these strange things, like that odd-looking fuzz on top of these heads? Do moths eat it? Will it keep?

That's what I meant by "housekeeping"—the reference early in our talk. Before I came to the Museum, I had experience in working at preparing material, but every kind of ethnological material has its own particular storage difficulties. Some of the pieces are fragile. Some are big. Some are made of materials like feathers that moths do eat. It's a question of having a rather flexible policy of care for the pieces, trying to keep the dust off and trying to keep them from being rubbed or crowded or whatever else might hurt them.

What are all those shell buttons lying over there? They look as if they were made out of abalone shell.

This is one of the restoring jobs that we are doing for the new hall. Part of the Maori collection from New Zealand consisted of a storehouse carved by native carvers, and it had shell insets for the eyes of the decorative figures. This was on exhibition in the hall for —let's see, it was 1907 when it came to the Museum, so it's been here quite some time. During this period some of the smaller visitors have pried out the shell insets, so in order to make the storehouse look as it did when we first got it, we're going to replace those eyes with shells similar to the ones that were removed.

Do you do that yourself?

The Department has a group of people who do work, specialized work, in restoring and preparing materials for exhibit.

But you do have to know whether the eyes are missing, and whether they ought to be put back, and what they ought to be made of?

That's right.

Thank you very much, Mr. Gifford. It seems to me, looking around this room, that you have quite a job on your hands. Where are you going to put all those spears and arrows?

One of the big problems in the whole area of museum storage is to get the pieces put away in such a manner that they can be used for study or can be seen, so that we can tell how many pieces we have and know just what types of materials we do have at any one time. It isn't a matter of piling them tightly in a box and closing the lid and locking it. All these things, like the spears, must be distributed in some way in the storage area so that they can be of value to visiting scholars or to people in the Museum who are working with them.

HARRY L. SHAPIRO

October 18, 1961

To reach the office of the Chairman of the Department, it is necessary to walk through a long office where two busy secretaries work, answer questions, and receive visitors. Dr. Shapiro's pleasant office also is a very deep room with tall windows at one end. His desk, piled high with periodicals and memoranda, stands between the windows, facing a very large bookcase, which almost closes off the darker end of the office with its seldom used door opening directly onto the corridor.

Very high cabinets line the two long walls. Behind the glass door of one of these is a set of photographs of the men who have been head of this department, the earliest at the top and Dr. Shapiro's picture—taken when he became head of the department in 1942—at the bottom. It is a custom followed by many scientists to acknowledge their scientific ancestry in this way. Other of the glass doors frame pictures of Indian life, a poster of an exhibition, and other reminders of Dr. Shapiro's interests and activities.

Dr. Shapiro, at this minute of the day, what are you doing? You're chairman of the Museum's Department of Anthropology. Are you administering?

I'm administering, yes. I try to do a little research in the short intervals between administering in the Department, and I also try to keep up with the advances in the science by reading the literature as much as I can, in what few moments I have.

What does administering a department like this mean?

Well, it means quite a variety of things. It means, first of all, planning a budget for the Department and maintaining all the activities for the Department. It means participating in committee work where policy and other things are discussed. It means being available and discussing with members of the staff their various problems that may arise.

It also takes in the problem of planning exhibits, which involves not only countless hours of solitary cogitation, hours of research, but also innumerable conferences with designers and the technical staff who build the exhibits. Then there is housekeeping, I mean storage, concern about collections—whether we have adequate collections or not, and if we don't, what to do about making them more adequate than they are. It means taking care of the small problems that come up in the life of a department like this, and they're so numerous and so varied that it's almost impossible to give you a complete list or description of all of them.

You yourself are a physical anthropologist?

I'm a physical anthropologist, which means, in simplest terms, the anthropology that is concerned with biological man, and this is traditionally a part of the larger concept of anthropology, although we do have our own bases of technique and data that differ somewhat from those used in other branches of anthropology.

What's the most interesting piece of fieldwork you ever did in physical anthropology?

That's a very easy one. That's the time I spent with the Pitcairn Islanders, who are the descendants of the mutineers of the *Bounty*. I really made two trips to visit these people. They're now divided into two colonies, one living on Pitcairn Island and the other on Norfolk Island. And I visited both islands and carried out researches in both communities, which came from the same mixture.

This was a genetic study, an attempt to study the effect of race-crossing, and also to get as much information as we could about the dynamics of a small, isolated community like this one.

Was that your first field trip?

My first trip, my first major field trip, was to Norfolk Island. Subsequently, much later, I went back to the group to make my study on Pitcairn Island. On the first trip I didn't get to Pitcairn Island for various reasons it would take too long to describe, but I did get back finally in the middle 1930's, and I visited Pitcairn.

How old were you when you went to Norfolk Island?

I was probably much too young. I think nowadays we would not recommend that people go off at that age. . . . I got a fellowship to make this trip when I was twenty and I started on the trip shortly after I was twenty-one.

You don't think people could go off nowadays . . . ?

Oh, I think they could, but nowadays the whole educational process has been expanded so much that we rarely feel that students are ready to do fieldwork at that age. Usually they're considerably older. I think this is simply part of the trend that students face nowadays. In my own case I do feel, as I look back on it now, that I should have had a little more preparation than I did have, but then perhaps one never has an adequate preparation for any problem.

If you had students you were thinking of sending out to do this problem now, how old do you think they ought to be and how much training do you think they ought to have today?

Well, I wouldn't put it on age, exactly. It would be a question of training. Let me put it this way: In 1923, which is very ancient history, when I went off on this first field trip, I was attacking a genetic problem. The amount of information that was available on human genetics, as I look back on it now, was very, very small. It wasn't anything like the field one would have to deal with nowadays. So the amount of training for a student going out today to do the same kind of problem would be very much greater.

And if he's going to do an up-to-date study, he's going to have to be familiar with all of the material that's been accumulated, all the genetic work that's been done in this general area. And much more has been done since 1923 than was done up to 1923. So from the point of view of background and training, a great deal more would be expected from someone going out nowadays to do the same kind of job than would have been possible at the time when I went out.

Can you tell what race people really belong to by looking at them?

I can, very often.

Are you ever asked to do it?

I am, frequently. I do quite regularly examine children for some of the adoption agencies where they have a problem of placement, and of course this has come up in rather dramatic ways.

Occasionally, aside from adoption problems, there

are other sorts of situations that human beings get themselves into that sometimes get taken to court, and I have acted as an expert in such cases.

In examining babies, this would mean that they belong to two races, wouldn't it?

Oh, sometimes more.

Sometimes three?

Sometimes three, and sometimes you can't tell how many. In a large metropolitan area like New York, many babies that come to the agencies have mixed racial backgrounds. Sometimes the agencies are not altogether certain about the racial background of the child and require some guidance in placing the baby.

What research problems are you interested in next, Dr. Shapiro?

I have a number of things that I'm working on. I'm particularly anxious to complete and publish some researches that I carried out in an earlier phase of my career that I haven't had the time to publish. I have some very interesting material on Chinese-Hawaiian race mixtures that I studied some years ago that's never been published, that I think is unique material.

I'm currently working on a problem that concerns the growth dynamics of the individual bones of the skull, and I've been working on that intermittently for the past year or so. I also have a very interesting sample of cranial material, that we obtained in the Marquesas, that may throw a great deal of light on the origin of the early Polynesians.

That's real bones you're talking about, isn't it?

These are real bones—skeletons, crania, and so on—that go back perhaps two thousand years.

All the other things you said were about live people?

About live people, yes.

IV

And If You Are a Professor

If your idea of what anthropologists do is based mainly on your visit to The American Museum of Natural History, it will appear to you that all their work is in some way connected with objects—spears and bowls, fossils and skulls, diagrams, maps, and photographs—and that their work cannot be done without tools of some kind, from calipers for measuring head forms to microscopes for examining textiles.

But if instead you begin your explorations into anthropology at Columbia University, your first impression will be a very different one. The Department of Anthropology is housed in Schermerhorn Hall, a staid, stone, copper-roofed building, which also houses many of the physical sciences, such as zoology and geology. Over its doorway is carved Job's admonition, "Speak to the earth and it shall teach thee."

At first glance, the anthropologists' offices show few signs of this spirit. Most of them are small and crowded —overcrowded—with books, and you may look in vain for objects such as spears or even for photographs of native peoples. The only pictures that you are likely to find are the ones in the Department office—framed photographs of former professors. It is difficult, in fact, to distinguish between these offices and others in a bookish department, French or Medieval History. As far as you can tell, anthropologists, like other university professors, spend their time teaching students out of books and writing more books for other professors to teach with.

However, by taking time to hunt around, you will discover some differences. Squeezed in among the offices, you will find the special departmental laboratories. One is for archeologists, where they spread out materials from a summer's dig for cataloguing and analysis. Another is for physical anthropologists; here students can handle specimens, human bones and fossils, so they will become familiar with them and learn to recognize them. There is also a darkroom, equipped for developing and processing still photographs from the field.

And then, if you sit for an hour or two in the Department office, listening quietly, you will hear fragments of conversations such as these:

"But if these boxes don't get off today, it will be three *months* before they get there!"

"My Urdu teacher has quit, and there isn't another one. What do I do now?"

"No, tell him he can *not* change the sequence. This isn't an art movie. This is real."

"He writes that the cockroaches eat right through an ordinary mosquito net. Doesn't sound very promising, unless we can live on a houseboat."

"But don't you realize? He's blind. He'll be using Braille paper for his notes, and that requires a different kind of paper clip."

"Silica gel is all very well for the film, but I'm going to try to keep the cameras dry with one of those new vacuum domes the Germans have just come out with."

"But it may take *two months* to get the visa for India. I can't wait till the grant comes through to ask for it. Otherwise, look at the field time I'll lose!"

"They want a projective test for people who have a poor sense of three dimensions. Any ideas?"

"Even if we send it air mail, it won't get there before they leave. There's all that long trip up the river."

"His original grant was for Cuba."

"I was joking when I said I'd expect to take a shower every day, and he took me seriously."

"I can't make up my mind whether to take my exams before or after the baby is born. But if I wait until after, there'll be so little time to plan for the field."

"But aren't you going to take anything at *all* to read, even if you are going by camel?"

Anthropology offices may be book-lined but, as often as not, anthropologists in the university, like their colleagues at the museum, are outward bound.

Once they arrive in the field, professors and students face the same conditions as museum curators. But graduate students, going to the field for the first time, have everything to learn—what kind of clothes, what kinds of cameras and tape recorders, which medicines will they need where they are going? They have a whole way of life to plan for, and often the only people whose advice they can ask have not seen the field site for many years.

Even if someone does remember accurately and has good descriptive notes about the site, conditions may have (in fact, almost certainly have) changed. Writing from a village on the Sepik River in New Guinea, which I last saw in 1938, a young collaborator of mine describes what it is like now. "The whole area is crowded," he writes, "with natives who have banded together to cut timber and hunt crocodile." Thinking back, I recall that the summer of 1938 was very dry, a good season for hunting. When the men of my village caught a crocodile, they would bring it home, cut it up, and smoke the chunks. Then as the meat got tougher and tougher, they would begin to quarrel and fling the leathery pieces at each other or out into the river. Nowadays crocodile are hunted for their hides, which are sold abroad to be made into women's shoes and handbags.

As on the Sepik River, the present situation may be very different from what it once was. All the information that the student is able to gather from earlier field workers and old monographs may be entirely out of date. Then too, there are the problems of assembling equipment—selecting the best new drug for malaria, finding where the strongest mosquito netting can be bought, deciding which typewriter is most sturdy, choosing between one tape recorder and another, each with its advantages.

The first step in organizing a field trip is deciding on a tribe and a problem. Sometimes one starts with a problem and finds a good place to study it. At other times one may start with an area—South America or Southeast Asia—and then decide on a problem and the best people to study.

The next step is finding out where to get funds to support the field trip. Once this has been decided, it is necessary to think through all the details that must be supplied on the information forms. And these also continually change. It will be necessary to find out, for example, what the *per diem* rate is—the amount of money that is allowed for everyday living expenses—for the island where the study is to be done. If it happens that this island is not listed in the United States government "permitted *per diem*" book, what is the closest equivalent to it? And what is the solution for the anthropologist if an agency has a rule that equipment must be bought through the local university? Such instructions are designed mainly for scientists who do research in laboratories; but what about the anthropologist who is going to the field? Finally, almost unexpectedly, all the choices are made and all the immediate problems are solved. His field trip organized, the student has advanced one more stage toward becoming an anthropologist.

Between field trips, professors and instructors teach, always with some awareness of the calendar. Anthropology is so small a profession that few of its members want just to teach and perhaps write an occasional article. Almost everyone works with one eye on his notes, figuring out how much he can get written up before the next trip and planning when and where that next trip will be.

Students often start their studies under one professor and complete them under a different one. It is from the continuous sense of movement—the planning and the organization and the writing up, in the relationship of these activities to "the field"—that students learn about being an anthropologist and have a chance to decide whether, after all, they would rather have a quiet five-day-a-week job, with their weekends free for a little reading.

In Appendix B, you will find short biographies of the department members on the Columbia University faculty who were interviewed over a span of many months. Since that time, one of them has died. Others, whose plans were only sketched or implied in our conversations, have completed these projects and moved on to new activities. Each of the biographies describes one or two of the person's special interests. Reading through these, you can easily turn to the interviews that appeal most to your own curiosity.

CONRAD M. ARENSBERG

March 31, 1962

Professor Arensberg, you're a social anthropologist, aren't you?

Yes.

What have you been doing today? What are you doing right now?

Today is given over mostly to lectures, and I'm lecturing about the Lapps in Norway and Sweden. They are reindeer hunters and they lead a special kind of life that we are eager to examine because it is in some ways like our own. They have small families, and they have teams of husbands and wives, and they have what is called bilateral kinship (that means they count relatives on both sides of the family as equally important), and they have some of the same social organization as we do ourselves.

They live in the woods and the forests and they herd reindeer, and you wouldn't expect that they would be organized in ways like ours or have the same kind of families as we who live in cities and work in factories and offices do. So the question in these lectures—and it meant a lot of discussion with the students in classes

—is, why are these people, these Lapps, like ourselves, when it seems that they ought to be doing something—particularly in their social organization—very different?

Professor Arensberg, what is the most interesting thing you've ever done in the past in your fieldwork?

In the past? I think maybe going out to a camp of Arabs one summer when it was very hot—out in Syria—when they moved in near a village. Visiting them and trying to work out for two days, or maybe it was three days, what their system of kinship relations was.

You worked in Ireland too, didn't you?

Yes, and one of my most interesting days there was when I climbed down from a high cliff to the shore of the ocean and found down there a very small beach, on which was drawn up a tiny boat, and by it was a big, wild-looking, tall man with red hair who spoke with a very foreign accent, not like the Irish brogue. For a wild moment I thought maybe he was German or Scandinavian, but then I remembered that he was probably speaking English from Gaelic, and it turned out that that was so. He only knew Gaelic, just a few words were in English, and he was from Arran Island, which was just visible offshore, about six miles out to sea through rather heavy waves. And before the day was over, he persuaded me, although it took a lot of persuasion, to go out with him in that small boat to the island six miles off. It was wet, and I didn't think we'd get there, and I saw myself as all kinds of a fool. But I went out there and it went very well indeed.

What are you most looking forward to doing next?

I want to go to India next. I hope to go there maybe next summer. And if not in the summer, then in my year off, a year from now. And there I want to go from the north, in the mountains, to the south, down on the jungle coast of Malabar, and see if I can make any sense of the different ways in which the people lay out their villages. I want to study their settlement patterns and their village organization. I know already that it changes. What I want to learn is how and why. That's what I want to do next.

Summer, 1964

Dr. Arensberg has just returned from a year in India, where he worked on his project and was in touch with several Columbia University students and alumni who also were doing fieldwork, Owen Lynch, Morton Klass, Lee Swartzberg, and Eleanor Wenkart, among others.

RUTH L. BUNZEL

November 11, 1963

Dr. Bunzel, you are Adjunct Professor of Anthropology at Columbia, is that right?

That's right.

And what are you doing this minute?

I am teaching and I'm very much involved in a group that's trying to get anthropologists working for peace in world affairs, and that takes up a great deal of my time.

What kind of group is that? Who is it made up of? What kinds of people?

It's made up of anthropologists. This is a follow-up of a resolution which was passed at the national meeting—to try and get some sort of consensus on anthropologists' attitudes toward world affairs that's comparable to the way they feel about race. Anthropologists have always taken a stand on race, and we're trying to find out if there's sufficient consensus for such a stand about disarmament, nuclear war, and so on.

That's what you're especially interested in right now, in addition to teaching. But you have done a great deal of fieldwork, haven't you?

Oh, yes, quite a long time ago.

What was your first field trip like? How old were you?

I had been out of college a few years. I had had a general course and a history major, and I had been in school for a long time and wanted to get out into the world, I thought, and so I had a couple of years in business. I didn't find that very rewarding and I was out of a job, so I went to work for Professor Boas. I hadn't had a course with him, though I had sat in on a course of his rather irregularly when I was an undergraduate, and I went to work for him as a secretary.

I became very interested in anthropology. And one year, when he was going to Europe, I had the summer off and thought I would use my vacation to go down to the Southwest, and I went with Ruth Benedict to Zuni. But before we went, Boas said, "Well, you know, if you're going down into a pueblo, you should do a job, a real piece of work."

I said I didn't think I was trained for work, and he said, "Well, you're interested in art, aren't you?" And I said, "Yes." And he said, "Well, do a project in art. Do a study of the relationship of the artist to her work." I thought that was rather a tall order. But I looked into some materials on this. And I went down, and I did a study of the relation of the artist to her work. When I came back, I found I was deeply interested in anthropology and decided that it was something that I could do, but that I had better get some training.

So I gave up my job and went back to school. I took two years at Columbia and a year at Chicago, and then started out with big jobs of fieldwork.

Well, now, what would you say today, after all these years of fieldwork, was one of the most interesting things that ever happened to you in the field?

Well, I think the year that I went back to Zuni knowing the language and really feeling that I belonged there and could participate in the culture. I felt that I really understood it. I think that was the most rewarding year. The years before, I had plugged away at learning the language and I had done jobs that other people had picked for me. But this was the problem which I had picked for myself.

What was the problem?

The individual in culture. It started as an attempt to get case studies—life-history material. Nobody had ever tried to collect life histories in a primitive society before, and I felt that this would be a way of finding out what it was really like to live as a Zuni. The culture fascinated me in its externals. There were many beautiful things about it, and I was always intrigued with what it must feel like to live this culture, and this is what I was trying to find out.

What are you thinking about as the most interesting thing you would like to be doing in the future? In addition, of course, to the work you are doing now on war and peace. Is this the future?

Well, it may be. But the thing I would really most like to do—I've done some work on Chinese culture with Chinese here—and the thing I would like most of anything to do would be to get back into Chinese work. Particularly on problems of perceptions of the world—cognition—how the people look at the world, how they see themselves and their environment.

I'm especially interested in this because the difficulties of communication with the Chinese, which have been so conspicuous in the past, seem to me to be in some way related to thought processes that are very different from ours. Many early writers on the Chinese have sensed this, but there has been no scientific work on it and so we still have these clichés about "the inscrutable Oriental."

HAROLD C. CONKLIN

November 8, 1963

Professor Conklin, you're in New Haven now, aren't you?

Yes, that's right.

What are you doing at this moment?

Well, we're still unpacking the three shipments that we made of notes and artifacts, and sorting various results of our fieldwork in Ifugao [the Philippines] last year.

You've just come back from Ifugao?

That's right—just a couple of months ago.

If you were to say what was the most exciting thing that you've ever done in the course of your work, what would you pick?

In terms of fieldwork that we did with the Ifugao?

Well, would that be it, or would it be some earlier field-work?

Well probably, in Ifugao—in terms of excitement, anyway—it was the feeling we had of belonging to a small group of kinsmen within our own little village on one night this last year, where there was a threat of attack from another community, and all the members of the community in which we were living, who were close kinsmen of each other, banded together immediately. We felt that we were very much participants in what tended to be, or looked like it would be, a real exhibit of a blood feud. I don't think I've ever participated in anything that was quite so exciting as that.

If that had really been a fight, what would you have done?

That remains to be seen (laughter)! We would have tried, I suppose, to keep out of the fray as much as we could have. It would have been very difficult, because we would have been associated with the people living in our immediate village.

In these feuds, do they attack women and children too?

No. Only men.

You had your wife and children there with you?

Yes indeed, but they would have been in the same position as all the other women and children in our village—they would have stayed at home and we men would have gone out to this other point where supposedly the encounter was to take place. Other encounters took place during the year, but this one was of major concern to about ninety-five per cent of the men in our village.

Now, if you look forward to the future—future fieldwork—what is it that you're most interested in doing next?

Comparing the results of this last year with other rice-farming communities in similar regions in the Mountain Province, and possibly other parts of the tropics in Asia.

Not entirely in the Philippines?

No.

When do you think you'll be doing that?

Not until after I've had a chance to write up the preliminary results of this last trip. It will be a good year or so.

And in between that you'll be teaching at Yale, too?

That's right.

Autumn, 1964

Dr. Conklin has managed to fit in a brief return trip to the Philippines this summer, between semesters at Yale University, for follow-up work with the Ifugao.

MORTON H. FRIED

June 29, 1962

Professor Fried, what are you doing right this minute that's related to anthropology?

Actually, I'm doing a number of things, and I suspect that most anthropologists find it difficult to do one thing at a time. In my case, it is a matter of teaching, trying to write, and at the same time assembling a project for the field.

Some years ago, before the Communist government was successful in taking over the Mainland, I did some work in China. Now I'm planning to go to Taiwan to continue some aspects of the study I made about fifteen years ago. Being particularly interested in the organization of the Chinese family and larger kinship groups, I intend to see how domestic groups in Taiwan compare with those I investigated in China. Of course, the basic population of Taiwan comes from China. Most of the people there are descended from forebears who migrated to the island two or three hundred years ago. I would like to see whether the passage of a few centuries has seen real divergence in the respective patterns of organization.

As a matter of fact, many specialists have long been dissatisfied with the common view that the Chinese prefer very large families. American students are often surprised to discover that the average size of the family in China is and has been between four and five members. This circumstance raises many questions.

To begin with, we may ask: Why should there be this difference between the actual size of Chinese families and what we *think* is the size? Why should some Chinese share the American misconception? These questions provide one of the problems, one of the things I am working on.

Professor Fried, you've really answered the question I was going to ask you third—which is what you're going to do next? So perhaps you'd like to say a little more about what you're doing right now, being an anthropologist today, besides planning for this new project?

Well, perhaps I jumped to the third question because I am not sure that my answers to the first two would be found sufficiently exciting. You see, most of my work at the present time consists of teaching and writing. I am preparing some general books and a few specialized articles based on previous work and reading.

When I go home this afternoon I'm going to apply myself once again to a small manuscript on evolution and culture. One focus of this particular work is on processes in the physical realm which may throw light on the processes of cultural evolution. Though evolutionary ideas about culture developed earlier than those applied to life, anthropology has been much influenced by ideas or models drawn from biology. The impact of Darwinian thinking has been so overwhelming that we have tended to overlook the fact that there is another aspect of the evolutionary process—that which goes into the making of elements, galaxies, and the cosmos. I believe that if we look more closely at what is being discovered about these processes, we may find profitable leads that can be applied to the study of culture.

Now, there's one other question I'd like to ask you. That is, can you describe one of the most exciting things that has happened in your anthropological past? I mean anthropologically, not just adventure.

Well, let me approach this by telling you what happened to an anthropologist friend of mine, Marshall Sahlins. He recently told me that the most exciting moment in his fieldwork came when he attended a party on the island of Moala, in Fiji, and was *not* given the place of honor.

Now this might sound strange, for certainly in the normal state of affairs in our culture someone coming to a party would *like* to be given the place of honor. Yet the working anthropologist begins to feel that he is really getting the confidence of the people among whom he is working when he is treated as a human being, and not simply as a symbol. It is one thing to be treated with respect because you've earned it, another to be regarded with awe and respect because you are a stranger from a powerful society.

The same thing happened to me in the town in China that I mentioned some time earlier. You may know that the Chinese are very, very particular about where everybody sits at a formal dinner, much more than we are. Well, I had the pleasure of sinking in the seating hierarchy until my actual place was in some relation to what I deserved.

But what really struck me as a single exciting moment occurred the day I walked down the main street of the small city in which I lived, the only non-Chinese in regular, continuous residence at that time. Instead of people saying such things as, "Here comes the foreign devil" or "Here comes the big nose," somebody leaned over and said, "Here comes the big bear!" He said it with a great deal of affection, referring to the fact that I, a portly type to begin with, was now bundled up in Chinese padded winter clothing. He didn't mind me wearing it. And I had the feeling that finally I was getting somewhere in local society.

Summer, 1964

Professor Fried will return to the Columbia University teaching staff this fall, after a year of research and seminar teaching in Taiwan.

JOSEPH H. GREENBERG

December 5, 1961

Professor Greenberg, what are you doing today?

At the moment I'm holding an office hour. Then I have a class in the history of anthropological theory. And after that I have a one-hour meeting with a young lady who is my secretary on a project called the West

African Languages Survey, of which I am the director. And then, when I get home, I will work on a revision of my book on the classification of African languages.

That's the work you'll be doing tonight when you get home?

That's right, yes, besides reading somebody's dissertation.

What's the dissertation on?

The grammar of Luo.

Where is Luo used?

Luo is spoken in Kenya.

Now, will you tell me something about one of the most interesting things you've ever done in the past?

Well, the basic idea which underlies the book I wrote, called *Essays in Linguistics*, came to me when I was in the New York Public Library one day when I was actually working on something else.

I had been dabbling around in mathematics, including set theory and theories of permutations and combinations. And suddenly it struck me that for a language, if we would take all the possible sets of permutations and combinations of sounds which constitute a language, then the grammar simply states which of these sets are permitted and which are not permitted. Therefore, in a sense, all grammatical theories can be considered a kind of analysis, in which you select the possible combinations among certain elements against those which do not occur. At the moment this struck me as an extremely exciting idea.

And what are you most looking forward to doing next?

I'm looking forward to my sabbatical year.

When is that?

Next year. What I'm interested in doing came out of a meeting which was sponsored by the Social Science Research Council Committee on Linguistics and Psychology, a meeting at which I was chairman, which was held in Dobbs Ferry in April of this year. The subject of this meeting was "Universals of Language," that is, what things are true of all languages.

For this meeting I did a paper myself, mostly on the problems of word-order elements in language. And what surprised me in doing this paper was that it ended more optimistically than I thought it would. That is, when I began it, I thought I would talk about it as a problem in method—and maybe end up with a discouraging statement that languages are so various that you can't find any general principle. The fact was, I came out with about fifty specific statements which could be checked in language, which, as far as I knew up to that moment, were true for all.

So what I would like to do during the coming year is to investigate problems of this kind in greater detail —not only questions of word order but other questions having to do with what is true in general about languages.

Professor Greenberg, some people are talking about the existence of so many languages as one of the things that interfere with peace. What do you think about our ever establishing a world language?

Well, if one means by that an auxiliary language which, for many people at least, will be spoken in addition to some other language or languages, it seems to me that we are in a sense already approaching the situation in which a very large proportion of the world's population speaks either English or French, these being the main contenders. So that, in fact, as most of us find in traveling, a knowledge of English and French is sufficient to take us most places.

I, for one, would not like to lose the main subject matter of my own study, and I also believe that along with other local peculiarities, language is one of the least harmful, in the sense you spoke of, and it helps to add to the variety and interest of the world.

But don't you think, when we say English and French are world languages, that's nice for you and me because we speak English, but what about people who don't speak either English or French as a first language? Aren't they worse off when English or French is the first language for a lot of other people?

There's no denying that. At the same time, we just have to face the situation in which, if we take very large language communities to begin with, like English and French, then we reduce the inconvenience, at least to a very large number of people. If we were to choose, for example, some language spoken in interior New Guinea as a world language, everybody would be in trouble except a very small number.

But everyone would be even, wouldn't they?

Yes, but this is not a question, to my mind, which is ever going to be solved by some kind of decree or decision. Attempts have been made, for example, with international languages like Esperanto, but they were artificial languages. They didn't have a well-assured base, to begin with. This is what prevented them from spreading. When you have a language spoken by millions of people, people will learn it because they know it will be valuable even if it doesn't take on as a world language.

It's kind of proof that it really works?

That's right. It's already useful to know it.

Summer, 1964

The manuscript Professor Greenberg went home to edit, that December evening, was published as Languages of Africa. *It is now going into its second edition. The work he presented at the Dobbs Ferry (N.Y.) meeting has appeared in the published report of that conference, which he edited,* Universals of Language.

RALPH S. SOLECKI

March 20, 1962

Professor Solecki, you're an archeologist, aren't you?

Yes.

Could you tell me what you're doing right now?

Right now, I've just finished advising on a doctoral dissertation—it took me about half an hour or more—on Mexican archeology. Then, just before that, I advised one of my staff members how to make out a travel log for his travels from the Sudan. He was on a Sudan archeological expedition for about three or four months and just returned, and he has to have his vouchers all turned in. And then another person came in regarding the proposed research he has on Neanderthals. He wishes to study the lower limbs of Neanderthals, and I advised him how to make out an application to the National Science Foundation.

That's Neanderthal Man?

Neanderthal Man. And I think we straightened out the outline of his budget, his plans, and everything to do.

And now tell me something about your own work. Tell me something about one of the most interesting and exciting things you've done in your own work.

Probably there were several things. Two things, I guess. One of them is my interest in the routes of early man, his migration from Siberia and Asia into North America. We've been tracing it up through northern Alaska, between the mountains and the sea. On the north slope of the Brooks Range, a distance of about ten miles from Peters Lake, we found some very early materials—crude flaked stone materials.

And the other was in the other program we have in northern Iraq, in the Zagros Mountain area, where we've been uncovering Neanderthal skeletons. Possibly one of the most interesting episodes was the discovery of our first Neanderthal skull.

In Iraq?

In Iraq, yes. It came as a surprise, something we didn't believe at first. But we had to believe it because it was there. It was a skeleton which had all the earmarks of a Neanderthal. It was laid in the proper context. And the first thing I envisioned was all the trouble and headaches this single individual was going to give us. A lot of worries, but very interesting ones.

What kind of worries was it giving you?

Well, one regarding the man himself—whether he was a "Classical" or a "Progressive" Neanderthal. Then, how he fitted into the scheme of the rest of the Neanderthal populations—his affiliations, the dating of the particular being. Also, one problem perhaps more sociological, and that is, he was a rehabilitated case. He had no right arm and he was evidently blind in the left eye. He seems to have been a crippled person—he couldn't move around very much—and apparently a person who was the object of compassion from the rest.

Would he have kept the fires going?

He would have kept the fires going. Oh, another thing. His front teeth were very much worn, so it would seem that perhaps he used his teeth to grasp, in lieu of his right arm.

How could you tell by his skull that something was wrong with one of his eyes?

We found extensive scar tissue along the left side of his face, right close to his eye, and our physical anthropologist, Dr. Stewart, has suggested that his left eye had been affected by a blow. He had been also struck rather severely on the right side of his head, because there is some extensive scar tissue on the skull.

Do you think this is the reason you found him in this intact state? Because he wasn't exposed to the same hazards as the others?

That could be, but we think actually that the truth lies elsewhere. The cave was situated in an earthquake belt, and it had been shaken. We think very likely his death is attributable to an earthquake. Stones were lying on his body and his bones were crushed. And I might add that his was not the only death from this cause. We found five other Neanderthals who had evidently been killed by rockfalls. The sixth, the only one that looked like a real burial, was a child.

What are you looking forward to doing next?

I'm looking forward to going back to Iraq to continue our investigations. That's in another year, 1963. We also have a program in the Sudan. This is in the Aswân area, where we are grubbing behind the new high dam, where the new reservoir will inundate a considerably larger area, and then up the river about three hundred miles. Our program deals with the prehistoric. I spent about a month there this past season overlooking the work.

This is part of saving things that will be lost forever, isn't it?

Yes, quite correctly. It's part of a salvage archeology program.

And that's what you're looking forward to most?

No, I'm looking forward more to the Iraq expedition.

You're going to both that year, then?

Well, I will advise on the Sudan project. We're going to be working with another organization on that.

What do you hope you'll find in Iraq next?

We expect to find more Neanderthals and also more information about them, that is, data concerning the climate and something about population.

It's usual to find a single Neanderthal, but to find a a population together makes a more interesting study, since this will give us a better insight into the problem of the two Neanderthal types. We'll know more about the range of variation within this race. Then we can make comparative analyses with other Neanderthal finds.

What do you do with these skeletons when they come back? Whom do they belong to?

They belong to the Iraqi government. They are part of the national antiquities. However, we have taken back for study at least two of the skeletons—to the National Museum, in Washington.

Summer, 1964

International complications made it impossible for Dr. Solecki to return to Iraq, for the time being, for further research on the Neanderthal remains at Shanidar Cave. Instead, he took a crew of Columbia University students to Syria, this summer, for a season of archeological research.

WILLIAM DUNCAN STRONG

December 5, 1961

Professor Strong, what are you doing just now, today?

Today is the office hour. I'll be here for two hours. I'll see students who are writing papers or writing doctoral dissertations or want some advice on anthropological problems.

Do you just sit here and they come, or do you make appointments?

We make appointments, and they just come too. They come by and see a light in the office and then come in. Many different kinds of problems come up. If you're chairman of a department, many kinds of technical problems come up. If you're not chairman, there's no telling what they may want. They may want to know about the latest date on fossil man in South Africa. They may want to know about the Incas of Peru. It might be almost anything.

And you tell them?

Well, I try. I can't say that I always come up with the right answers, but I can tell them where to go to look, references either in the Museum or at the library.

Now Professor Strong, you are both an archeologist and an ethnologist, aren't you? And you're listed in the Columbia catalogue as giving a course this term on the ethnology of the American Indians. What's your background for this?

Of course, I was trained in anthropology, and that includes archeology and ethnology and physical anthropology. Linguistics, too. At least that's the way it's done in the United States. So you have to have a background in all of those. As a matter of fact, I've done fieldwork in ethnology in the Great Plains, in Labrador, in Peru. Archeology in many places. I've done physical anthropology in Labrador. In fact, we're all called on to do all sorts of things, and we have to be ready to do them.

What do you think of as your field?

I would say cultural anthropology, which is a combination of the first three. Physical anthropology is something I'm willing to do, but I really have the background for cultural anthropology.

When I said "field" this time, I meant on the map. Doesn't every anthropologist have a place on the map, or two or three places, that he likes better than any other?

Yes, I see. There I would say Peru or Central America. But I've also been fascinated with the Great Plains. On the Great Plains you found out that you couldn't understand ethnology unless you had archeology, unless you knew what had happened out there earlier and heard the people speaking about what happened. And the two studies, ethnology and archeology, could be dovetailed.

Now, what is one of the most interesting things you ever did in your fieldwork? Not* the *most interesting thing but* a *most interesting thing?

Well, you take an exciting time like finding the tomb of a warrior-god down in Peru. They had buried an old, old man who apparently had been a god, a priest, when he was alive. There were god masks—one had great carved fangs—showing the mythology of the time. It showed how he had served as an agricultural god. Then, right alongside him, there was a warrior's staff with an engraved background, a carving that showed things exactly like those in the tomb with him. It was heavy, with a round copper point on it which he had used in fighting. It was all battered. He was obviously a great chief and priest. And there was this other long, elaborately carved piece of wood, about six feet long, a digging stick with an owl carved on the top of it. Apparently from some bird cult.

And all these things were preserved. The whole carving on the staff showed the man who had been buried, down to the last details of the dress. This piece also showed the figure of a small boy alongside the priest. Then, when we dug further, there it was—the skeleton of a small boy, just as in the carving. It was an exciting time.

When was this?

This was in 1946.

Now, what are you going to do next? Have you decided?

Well, the trouble with archeology is that you get all blocked up. There's a tremendous amount already dug, and it takes a long, long time to write up archeological material. We're working a good deal on much of our old stuff. In the meantime we have some very exciting things going on in Mexico and Guatemala. This summer I intend to go down and see what's happening there, and perhaps later . . .

We're always sending people out to different parts

of the world—up to the Eskimo country, or out to the South Seas, or down to South America or Central America. Working with these people is always exciting—to see what they do.

So at the moment you have groups of students placed out around the world and you're thinking of what they're doing?

Of the people out in the field, yes.

Summer, 1964

It is at death that a man's measure is taken. William Duncan Strong (Dunc, to his many friends) died less than two months after this interview. His impress on American anthropology is permanent, through his students, many of whom are now leading figures in the field, through the many anecdotes and near-legends surrounding his work on the Great Plains, with the Naskapi Indians, and in Peru, but essentially, of course, through his work.

His bibliography, published in the American Anthropologist *(October, 1963), contains more than one hundred titles. Several of these are prophetic; others are landmarks in the synthesis of archeology and ethnology that was his own pioneering contribution.*

CHARLES WAGLEY

January 9, 1962

Professor Wagley, what are you doing today?

Well, today has been and will be, I imagine, a rather typical day. I finished my lecture to my graduate class. It's toward the end of the semester, so I'm summing up a course on the social organization of primitive people. Today, I talked about the different types of social organization found over the world.

And then I had lunch with my colleagues—with you, Ruth Bunzel, Duncan Strong, Conrad Arensberg, Joseph Greenberg, and others of this department. We joked and gossiped about other anthropologists, and we also discussed the problems of our department.

I'll have to give about two hours to administrative work this afternoon, connected with the new Institute of Latin American Studies at Columbia University.

And then, from four to six, I have my graduate seminar. I'm rather looking forward to that, because an outside speaker will come to talk to us about the Latin American novel and how the anthropologist might get new insights into Latin American culture by reading fiction.

Professor Wagley, could you tell me one of the most interesting things that happened to you in the past?

I suppose among many would be the day that I first arrived, afoot, in the Tapirapé village in central Brazil. I had been traveling by canoe—first by truck and then canoe—some ten to fifteen days. I was one of two or three of the first Westerners to enter into the village, and I found them in the midst of one of their most important festivals. It characteristically took place all afternoon and they danced all night.

I was very tired, having walked some thirty-five miles that day, but I tried to stay up all night to write down in my notebook everything that happened. Of course, it being the first day, I didn't understand a thing that I saw. About five o'clock in the morning I dozed off for an hour or so, and about a month or two later I found out that I had missed the most important event of the night.

What was it?

This was a great giveaway ceremony, in which the men of prestige accept the challenge—by drinking a nonalcoholic beverage—of the people of less prestige. This means that the man must give away practically all of his property—his beads, his parrot feathers, and his other ornaments. But during the year these same goods, values, come back to him and to others, because this is a gift-giving society.

Professor Wagley, what are you looking forward to most within the next few years?

Well, all anthropologists say and feel that they would like to do fieldwork, but at this time it seems to me that fieldwork for me is changing. I'm very interested in making use of my knowledge and what more materials I can gather, for the development of what might be called inter-American relations. I think the anthropologist has a great deal to contribute, and through the mechanism of our new Institute at Columbia University, through writing, lecturing, it seems to me I could be most useful in that sphere.

And when you say the contribution of anthropology to international affairs, what do you mean?

I mean that anthropologists, in a sense, can explain and help the understanding of different behavior, which is important at the negotiation table. It is important in person-to-person relationships between people of different nations, and it is important in understanding the motivations, the desires and aspirations of other people. They may not be ours or similar to ours.

Summer, 1964

Professor Wagley's new book, An Introduction to Brazil, *published late in 1963, has been acclaimed by reviewers and men in public life for accomplishing an important step toward the goal he has set for himself and for the Latin American Institute of Columbia University, which he directs; that is, the furtherance of inter-American relations through the development of new areas of understanding, in this case, with the people of Brazil.*

V

In My Office

In planning this book I decided to include an interview with myself, partly because I am interested, about equally, in teaching and in museum work, and partly because my office is a crossroad for many of the kinds of activity that go on in anthropology. Then, too, I am supposed to be writing this book and there is a limit to the time I can ask my colleagues to give up—even though, as I explained to them, all the proceeds of the book will go to anthropological research. Of course, it would be too artificial to ask myself questions, but I shall try to write as if a group of students were here in the office with me, looking around and asking questions.

To begin as in the interviews, here at the Museum I am Curator of Ethnology. At Columbia University I am Adjunct Professor in the Department of Anthropology. In 1925, just before I sailed for Samoa on my first field trip, Dr. Pliny Earle Goddard, the Museum's Curator of Ethnology, asked whether I would be interested in a job at the Museum. He said someone was needed to help Americans understand cultural anthropology as well as they then understood archeology. That was the year that Roy Chapman Andrews brought back dinosaur eggs from the Gobi Desert, and everything ancient stirred public interest. People were talking about prehistoric American mound builders; the British excavations in Athens; the lively dispute over King Tutankhamen's tomb in Egypt; and Turville-Petre's tremendously exciting find in Palestine —the first Neanderthal skeleton discovered outside Europe. But Dr. Goddard could only sound me out. He could not formally offer me the job because Dr. Clark Wissler, Chairman of the Department, was in Australia, helping to set up a new department of anthropology at the University of Sydney.

Of course, I said yes. When I first went into anthropology, there was no real hope for a job. I thought I would have to make my living by working as a school psychologist. And there was little prospect of money for fieldwork, except for very short trips to American Indian reservations. However, in 1923, the year I graduated from Barnard College, the National Research Council provided a new group of fellowships, and it was on one of these that, two years later, I was setting out for Samoa to study the adolescent girl in a primitive setting.

One day about midway in my field trip, a cable came offering me the Museum job. I remember that there was no one to understand what it meant and no way to celebrate. I just walked away along the beach, alone, thinking what it would be like. Returning from Samoa, I came by way of Europe. The Museum had given me time to attend my first big international congress—the twenty-second meeting of the International Congress of Americanists, which was held in Rome. The members of the Congress were received by Mussolini, and the city was filled with Fascist guards—to protect Mussolini, not to protect us.

When at last I arrived home and came to the Museum, it was explained that there was no real office free for me. I would have to take a kind of cataloguing room up in the sixth floor tower, where old Mr. Sabine sat putting numbers on specimens of new collections. I was next to youngest of the department members (Dr. Shapiro was the youngest)—and I was a girl. Dr. Wissler used to say that museum work fitted women because it was rather like housekeeping. And, in fact, most of the "housekeeping" then was done by Miss Bella Weitzner, who came to the Museum straight from high school and later was appointed to the scientific staff. When she retired, she was Associate Curator of Ethnology.

This office, when I moved into it, was a bare place.

This desk was here—one of the old rolltops with a top that rippled down. I had that top sawed off for my fiftieth birthday. There were six low tin cabinets, painted white, and empty. The only other furniture was one bookcase, two chairs, and one big table. Even the walls were bare until I hung up mats and pieces of bark cloth and maps of the world. Erich Schmidt, the Middle Eastern archeologist who later was at the Oriental Institute of the University of Chicago (and who led the Persepolis expedition in the 1930's) had just come to this country and the Museum had given him an office even smaller than mine across the hall. He and I used to stand poring over the maps, discussing where we wanted to go next.

Slowly, over the years, this room has filled up. In 1928, while I was in the field, Miss Weitzner wrote to me that an office had become vacant on the fifth floor, where all the other curators are, and that I was to be moved down there. But I wrote back begging to be left up in my tower. By that time I had learned that I could get a lot more work done up here, out of the way. Being a woman, I was not paid as well or advanced as fast as the men in the Department, but I did have a lot of freedom to do as I liked.

At one time a lot of tall wooden cupboards suddenly became available because no one knew what to do with them. Probably someone else, somewhere else in the Museum, was having new metal cabinets made. I was away on a field trip, but someone decided to have them put up here, lining two walls of the office. These eight cupboards, lining the east wall, are now filled with files of my books and reprints. The four against the south wall hold reprints, very old field notes, and photographs. These beautiful steel bookcases against the west wall were another unsolicited gift of furniture that nobody knew what to do with, and once they were put in, there was no more empty wall space at all. In fact, to find room for books, we have built shelves up against the ends of the cabinets.

My office arrangements are a little odd. I use what is actually an outer office, while my secretaries have the inner one. This is because their office used to be a storeroom where Peruvian gold was kept, together with lots of odds and ends. The label on the door read "Unidentified Specimens." For a time, in the early 1940's, someone let a musicologist work there—so that his phonograph records would not disturb anyone else. And once, in 1941, I got permission for Claire Holt to use the room while she was analyzing our collection of hundreds of little wooden Balinese carvings. But even then only a tiny space was cleared. Around the curve of the tower were skeletons and old full-scale models of Indians.

After World War II, I was finally given the use of this inner room, but I stayed in the outer office. Anthropologists don't care very much about status, and we all know how to type. I can always pretend that I am my secretary and go on typing.

Now we also have the little office across the hall for one of my projects—a study of how different peoples orient themselves in time and in space and how they react toward the unknown and the strange. This project is directed by my colleague, Rhoda Metraux, who has her desk in an alcove around the curve of the tower, next to a collection of Chinese pots and with a window looking west toward the Hudson River. I can retire there, too, when I want to write uninterruptedly.

As you see, we are terribly crowded. On top of the cabinets we store back files, and those gray boxes on top of the bookcase by the door are full of prints of pictures of Balinese children, the ones we processed but did not use in *Growth and Culture,* a study of Balinese childhood. Above the cabinet on the south side are packages of children's drawings, brought back from Bali by Jane Belo, and a bundle of photographic enlargements made for a special Balinese exhibit in the Museum of Modern Art. There is also a bundle of photographs of the Manus, some taken in 1928 and others in 1953. I have studied the Manus twice—once when they were a primitive people and again when they had come into the modern world. We made the enlargements for the Museum's CBS television show *Adventure,* so the audience could see how much they had changed. And in one cabinet are all the notes from my first six field trips (Samoa in 1925, Manus in 1928, an American Indian tribe in 1930, Arapesh in 1931, Mundugumor in 1932, and Tchambuli in 1933)—notebooks, negatives, prints, maps, catalogues, in fact, everything.

In those earlier years, you could take only as many pictures as you could develop the same night. There were no movie cameras or tape recorders, and no flashbulbs you could depend on for taking pictures at night. Once we carried a hundred big flashbulbs for two days on a mountain trail, only to find that not one of them worked. And once, in 1936, we took to Bali a dictaphone with batteries that required recharging. But by the time we had arrived in the mountains, the batteries had leaked and were useless. All this meant that our field notes were less voluminous. Most recording was done with the anthropologist's pencil and only about two years at home were needed to write up one year's field notes. Besides, since our ideas of fieldwork were much more simple, our notes were less detailed and we wrote them up more simply.

During my first year at the Museum, in 1926, I wrote my first book, *Coming of Age in Samoa,* and started to revise the Maori exhibit in one of the two halls for which I was responsible. This was on display in the tower room, which we are using now to work on the new Peoples of the Pacific Hall. I also wrote a little guide for the revised collection.

During my first winter, I also served as assistant in Ruth Benedict's anthropology course at Barnard College. Each week the Barnard students came down to the Museum and were shown through a different hall. This meant that I had to learn a great deal more about these halls than I had learned when I myself was taken through them as a Barnard senior.

That summer I went to Europe to visit every museum in Germany. I looked over their South Seas' artifacts and made sketches of interesting specimens of types lacking in the collections in our Museum. The whole trip, including tourist-class passage on a ship and third-class travel by train across Germany for seven weeks, cost $425. Theodore Schwartz, my young colleague who is now out in New Guinea selecting a site for our new fieldwork, made a similar trip last winter. But he was equipped with a Leica camera and fast film, and he traveled by plane. In little more than three weeks, he looked at collections in museums in Germany, Switzerland, and Holland, and he brought back enough photographs and microfilms, tightly packed in folders, to fill over a yard of file cabinet space.

The second winter at the Museum, I wrote a technical monograph on Samoa; this was published by the Bishop Museum in Honolulu. But I had, as yet, no publisher for my first book. I had taken the manuscript to Harper and Brothers, and after a decent interval they had sent it back to me. I didn't know what to do next. I had written the book in ordinary English because it seemed to me that the people who really needed to know something about adolescence in a faraway primitive culture were unlikely to have an elaborate anthropological vocabulary and would not want to read a book studded with Samoan words.

It was customary, in those days, in books by anthropologists, to use a great many native terms. A page of a monograph often looked like this:

> The dancers (or societies) are arranged in two principal groups, whose names among the Kwa-

> kiutl proper are the seals (mē'êmqoat) and the quē'qutsa. The former embrace a number of dancers and societies of dancers—the hā'matsa, ha'mshamtsEs, k·înqalaLala, nō'ntsîstalaL, qoē'-qoasElaL, q'ō'minōqa, nā'nē, nū'LmaL. They are the highest in rank. All the others are quē'qutsa. . . .
>
> The Nā'q'oaqtôq are divided as follows: The group corresponding to the seals are called wu'-n'awunx·îs, the troublesome ones. They embrace hāmats'a, bear, and mā'maq'a. I have not a complete list of the subdivisions of the quē'qutsa.
>
> L'ō'L'Epana (cormorants) are the chiefs, ēsElā-liLtsawē qoayî'm (the whales for whom one waits), are the young men, ts'ē'ts'eg·inaqa (gulls), the elder boys.
>
> The group corresponding to the seal group is called among the Koskimo ts'E'qolag·ilîs, and embraces wolves and hā'mats'a. The chiefs among this tribe are called t'ō't'opa (rock-cods), and the higher chiefs nā'nē (bears). The middle-aged men are called guē'gusō (pigs).*

The style of *Coming of Age in Samoa* did not fit into this monograph pattern. I had written it as a book which could be understood by schoolteachers, psychologists, and parents.

In those days, all the anthropologists in New York

* Franz Boas, "The Social Organization and the Secret Societies of the Kwakiutl Indians," *Report of the U.S. National Museum for the Year Ending June 30, 1895* (Washington, 1897), pp. 419–20.

used to meet once a week for lunch. Recently we had been joined by a spry little man named George Dorsey. He had been for many years a perfectly conventional ethnologist, who wrote long technical accounts of Plains Indian sun dances and descriptions of Skidi Pawnee Indian life. Then, quite suddenly, Dorsey gave up the scholarly life of museum work and married a young wife. He also took a trip around the world. From this, he came back greatly impressed with the work of the great Russian physiologist Pavlov, and, full of enthusiasm, he wrote a book, *Why We Behave Like Human Beings,* which was intended for the educated layman. It was a tremendous success. Dorsey moved into a penthouse, bought two beautiful Chinese rugs, and began to feel expansive.

It was Dorsey who sent me to Harper with my manuscript, and he also suggested the title, *Coming of Age in Samoa.* Untroubled by the failure of this first venture, he continued to keep my problem in his nimble mind as he whirled through New York literary life, going to lunches and cocktail parties as most successful authors did then—and still do. (Fortunately, I usually have been away in the field when my books have appeared. So I never had to attend a publisher's party given for me until 1959, when a book I wrote for young people, *People and Places,* was published. This time the publisher had been so generous in planning for illustrations that I felt I should do whatever was asked of me.)

One day, at a literary luncheon, Dorsey sat next to

William Morrow, who had just started a new publishing firm. When Dorsey learned this, he began to grumble about the treatment of my Samoa manuscript—which is one way of getting other people interested. Mr. Morrow, in turn, wondered whether this might not be a book for a new house. Of course, Dorsey sent me to see him. Mr. Morrow had dealt with educational books all his publishing life, and when he had read the manuscript (which then ended with the final chapter on Samoa), he asked me: "What would you have to say if you wrote some more about what all this means to Americans?"

Fortunately, I knew. When I came back from Samoa I was asked to give lectures before an assortment of audiences—in schools, in the Long Island town where a cousin lived, in a new housing project for intellectuals—and, when I was asked about the meaning of what I had found in Samoa, I was compelled to think through the answers. It seemed clear, to start with, that if girls in Samoa did not have to live through the difficulties that face American girls in adolescence, then the problem is not the inevitable, universal one that it was assumed to be. If one society could bring its children through adolescence painlessly, then there was a chance that other societies could do so also. What then, audiences wanted to know, did this mean to us, as Americans? During the same winter, I was also teaching an evening class of working girls, and their questions, which I had to answer, were quite different from those I had thought of.

Fresh from these experiences, I was ready to write the last two chapters—one comparing the lives of Samoan and American girls and one called "Education for Choice." This chapter, written in 1928, is still relevant. The problem of bringing up children who are free to choose among many alternatives is one we shall be trying to solve, in new and better ways, as long as we are a democracy.

The manuscript was at last complete. Then, once more prodded by Dorsey, I asked Professor Boas to write a preface for the book—which he did. It went to press, I read proof, and saw a small printer's dummy of the table of contents, chapter one, and the jacket. This done, I sailed for Hawaii, glad to be on my way to the field in the Admiralty Islands.

For this field trip, I had a Social Science Research Council fellowship to study little children in a project which, without humor, had to be called "a study of the thought of the *preschool* child in the Admiralty Islands" even though there had never been a school in Peri, the village where I did my work. When I had been in the field about four months, a letter came from my publisher telling me that *Coming of Age in Samoa* was a success. It was a good time to be away. In the United States, when too-early success comes to writers, we very often ruin their chances of doing anything else.

In any case, writing those last two chapters was invaluable. From this experience I learned that, for me, the way to write a book which will make the life of a remote island people meaningful to an American audience is to lecture about it first—lecture to all kinds of audiences—in schools, before scientists' groups, and in women's clubs, in as many parts of the country as possible, before I even begin to write. And I have done so. Since World War II, I have spent two or three weeks every winter in California, lecturing sometimes several times a day, so I can be sure of having some idea of what far-western audiences are thinking.

During the war, in 1943, I was sent to England to try to explain Americans to the English. There, too, I was able to try ideas out in lectures and over the British radio before I wrote a pamphlet for the British and the American troops. This explained, among other things, what I had learned about the differences in dating behavior in Britain and in the United States. In our country, the girl was expected to say no—and make it stick; in Britain, the boy was expected not to ask casually—and so his asking was taken seriously. And, of course, the differences between these two patterns had led to a lot of confusion and unhappiness in the relations of American boys and British girls.

Coming back to the present, in this office, the deep drawers in the end cabinet also are filled with things from old projects. One drawer contains the beautiful analytical cards on the Balinese carvings made by Claire Holt before she left, in 1942, to teach Malay (the language which today is known as Bahasa) to classes of servicemen, who would one day be part of the occupation forces in the Pacific.

Below that drawer are the files of a study dating from 1940–41, a project which had to be interrupted soon after Pearl Harbor when, with so many men needed for the war, social science research in hospitals and medical schools came to a halt. This project, "The Family Study," was the first one in which the skills of doctors, nurses, and social workers were combined to deepen the understanding of a sick person by placing him in the setting of his family. While this study was going on, I was called in as a consultant to help place families in the larger context of the culture. This meant, for example, explaining that a Jewish patient, who let his wife work while he himself spent the day studying the Talmud, was acting in a way that was appropriate to the behavior patterns of Eastern European Jews. Or that a Hungarian war veteran with a stomach ulcer would prefer surgery to having his wife feed him from little jars of baby food. This project was written up by Dr. Henry B. Richardson in his book, *Patients Have Families.*

After the wartime interruption, new studies of this kind got under way. Today, about twelve per cent of the anthropologists working in the United States are doing research in hospital settings—studying hospitals as they have learned to study villages, or interpreting the cultural backgrounds of the different patients so that their hopes and fears can be better understood by doctors and nurses, or helping to equip medical students and residents to treat the tremendous variety of patients who come to clinics and doctors' offices. I myself now spend two weeks every winter at the Department of Psychiatry of the University of Cincinnati College of Medicine and, at eighteen-month intervals, I spend six weeks at the Menninger School of Psychiatry in Topeka, Kansas.

In still another drawer of the same cabinet are files from studies made in the mid-1930's. One, carried out in 1934, was a project in which people from several fields—psychology, psychiatry, human biology, philosophy, anthropology, and sociology—met together for a summer month at the Hanover Inn near Dartmouth College, in an attempt to outline all we then knew about how human beings develop from birth to adulthood.

This marked the beginning of a new and fruitful kind of interdisciplinary work. Nowadays, I sometimes spend as many as sixty days a year in conferences with specialists from other fields of science and from other countries, developing new ideas about how to study or solve some problem. The kinds of problems dealt with in this way range very widely: How the ideas of information theory and "feedback" can be applied both to the processes going on in one organism and in a whole society; how we can combine our knowledge of animal behavior with what we know about human behavior; how we can understand and define consciousness; how we can pool in a single science all we know about how people communicate—with words, with grunts, with gestures, even with silences; how we can best apply all we know about speed of change in a whole society to the problems of change that are springing up all over the world. And this now familiar interdisciplinary approach to social science problems goes back to that summer in 1934, when Lawrence K. Frank brought a group of us together in the Hanover Conference.

At that conference I also learned, through Lawrence Frank, what a tremendous role private foundations like The Rockefeller Foundation, the Carnegie Corporation of New York, the Josiah Macy, Jr. Foundation, and more recently, The Ford Foundation (and, of course, many others) have played in the development of American science and education and may, perhaps, play in the future of the world. One brilliant, courageous, imaginative man, working for a foundation with hundreds of thousands and even millions of dollars to spend, can start ideas on paths that will open up for decades. But equally, one stupid, conventional, opinionated, or simply unimaginative man can block development in a science by giving too much money to the wrong kind of research.

Today, a very great part of the support given to anthropological research comes from the federal government—from the National Science Foundation, the National Institutes of Health, and other government bodies. But for the support of some very new and speculative ideas we still depend, as we did in the past, on foundations, with their greater freedom to meet the challenges of unusual risks. The social sciences, unlike the natural sciences, enter very immediately into the lives of all kinds of people. For this reason social-science research is also more open to challenge and criticism. One of the tasks of the anthropologist is to fit social research into the deep preferences of a culture so that foundations, government bureaus, and federal agencies can support the different kinds of work that need to be done.

Several parallel studies followed on the Hanover Conference in the mid-1930's. One, known as "The Adolescent Study," tried to take a new look at the problems faced by high-school students—not only boys and girls in high school but also younger ones just coming to high school and older ones going on as freshmen in college. In another project, an attempt was made to rethink courses of study in science, literature, and mathematics in a program which was designed to revolutionize teaching methods in the whole country. Unfortunately, these proposals were published just at the beginning of World War II, when no one had time to put ideas of this kind into effect. Instead, American education got more and more behind the times until, very suddenly, with the launching of Sputnik, people woke up and demanded that something be done. Ironically, the kind of change people now demanded was just what the Progressive Education Association (which had carried out the earlier studies) had asked for in the 1930's—that we really teach our students up to the level of their intelligence, free from the binding ideas of dated, meaningless work.

This huge, flat steel file, standing in the center of

my office, is a map file. But we have found a new use for its very wide, shallow drawers. In every one we have stored big sheets of white cardboard, on each of which are mounted enlargements of a single roll of Leica film. Arranged in this way, the file stores 20,000 photographs from my last field trip to the Admiralty Islands in 1953. Anyone who knows the pictures well can go through the whole file in about four hours to pick out the ones that are wanted for a book or an article. This is possible because, today, with modern processing, enlargements can be made with automatic controls.

But in 1939, when we came back from the field with 38,000 stills, the best we could do was to have filmstrips made of the Leica rolls; and then, to find specific pictures, we had to look at the strips, one by one, through a filmstrip projector. Working every evening, it took us the whole summer of 1941 to go through 26,000 pictures in order to choose the 5,000 we thought we might use for our book, *Balinese Character: A Photographic Analysis.* But this was only the first step. After this, my husband, Gregory Bateson, had to enlarge all 5,000 pictures; from these we finally selected the 759 actually used in the book.

Such hard work would not be necessary today. It takes far less time to scan enlarged pictures pasted up on a cardboard mat—and someone else can do the pasting. That "someone" is often an anthropology student who has learned how very crucial it is to get each picture exactly in place and who realizes that a picture lost in 1963 may cause havoc in 1983. And most of the work in my office—checking slides and negatives, packing for field trips and checking spare parts, making out bibliography cards or identifying specimens—is done by future anthropologists who already understand how important it is to get things right in every detail.

And here, against the east wall, in these steel bookcases which I inherited from some other office, are the field notes from my later field trips, volume after volume of typed-up materials, all recorded on a precise time grid so that moving pictures, stills, tapes, and native texts for a given time of a specific day can be taken out and easily fitted together.

On both sides of the shelves of notes are clusters of books—packed close on the shelves, but still arranged into groups. Some are arranged by area—Polynesia, Melanesia, Mexico, West Africa, Russia, France, Germany—because anthropologists always think about actual people, who can be located on maps, in the kind of place they really live in. Other books are grouped by the subjects on which I, as an anthropologist, have worked with other specialists in nutrition, education, child care, child psychology, mental health, urban planning, family life, religion, and animal behavior.

In the inner office, surrounded not by a clutter of "unidentified specimens" but by working files and shelves that rise to the high ceiling, three or four students almost always are at work. Here are the records, bound in notebooks and stored in files—more than half a ton of them—of projects that came out of World War

II and have continued over many years, the national-character studies. This form of anthropology, which was first developed in response to wartime needs, evolved further through new peacetime uses; for example, in connection with the worldwide technical assistance programs undertaken by United States' federal agencies and by the United Nations. Through these studies, patterns of behavior are identified as characteristic of a people—Russians, Germans, Frenchmen, Czechs, Thais, Poles, Syrians, Chinese, or Japanese, and so on—in a variety of situations—in victory, under siege, in defeat, as friends or rivals, in relations with new nations and old ones, in disaster, or in times of change.

Here also are the records of a number of smaller projects, such as one undertaken in the 1950's by the Society for Applied Anthropology for the International Motion-Pictures Division of the United States Department of State, and a more recent one done for the Outdoor Recreation Resources Review Commission. Here, too, are the working copies of films from all the field trips since 1936—collections of photographs and rolls of Leica film.

The main reason an office like this one becomes so crowded is that here no material is ever dead. Nothing can be spared to be carted off, neatly boxed, to some remote basement. Tomorrow morning I may urgently need a list of the people around the world who worked on primitive childhood in 1949, or the notes for a project on Fiji I designed in 1934, or the unpublished notes on an Arapesh bark painting I copied in watercolor while the artist was making it in 1931.

In anthropology everything is quite literally related to everything else. Nothing one has ever seen or heard, smelled or tasted, is meaningless or unconnected with other things. One's working life and one's personal life, life out in the field and in the office, life down the hall and in a small village in Europe—all these interlock. This is why anthropology is a particularly good career for people who see and remember and enjoy discovering unexpected connections, who expect to find life all of a piece.

VI

A Day in the Field

There are different ways of describing an anthropologist's day in the field. One way is to trace the activities of the working ethnographer as closely as possible as he moves through the day. Another is to describe what may be considered a fairly typical day in the life of the people. In *Coming of Age in Samoa,** I chose the second method, with the idea of giving readers some sense of the tone and the pace of life as I had experienced it.

I am reproducing this description to show you what I mean.

* Copyright 1928 © 1955 by Margaret Mead.

A DAY IN SAMOA

The life of the day begins at dawn, or if the moon has shown until daylight, the shouts of the young men may be heard before dawn from the hillside. Uneasy in the night, populous with ghosts, they shout lustily to one another as they hasten with their work. As the dawn begins to fall among the sofa brown roofs and the slender palm trees stand out against a colorless, gleaming sea, lovers slip home from trysts beneath the palm trees or in the shadow of beached canoes, that the light may find each sleeper in his appointed place. Cocks crow, negligently, and a shrill-voiced bird cries from the breadfruit trees. The insistent roar of the reef seems muted to an undertone for the sounds of a waking village. Babies cry, a few short wails before sleepy mothers give them the breast. Restless little children roll out of their sheets and wander drowsily down to the beach to freshen their faces in the sea. Boys, bent upon an early fishing, start collecting their tackle and go to rouse their more laggard companions. Fires are lit, here and there, the white smoke hardly visible against the paleness of the dawn. The whole village, sheeted and frowsy, stirs, rubs its eyes, and stumbles towards the beach. "Talofa!" "Talofa!" "Will the journey start to-day?" "Is it bonito fishing your lordship is going?" Girls stop to giggle over some young ne'er-do-well who escaped during the night from an angry father's pursuit and to venture a shrewd guess that the daughter knew more about his presence than she told. The boy who is taunted by another, who has succeeded him in his sweetheart's favor, grapples with his rival, his foot slipping in the wet sand. From the other end of the village comes a long-drawn-out, piercing wail. A messenger has just brought word of the death of some relative in another village. Half-clad, unhurried women, with babies at their breasts, or astride their hips, pause in their tale of Losa's outraged departure from her father's house to the greater kindness in the home of her uncle, to wonder who is dead. Poor relatives whisper their requests to rich relatives, men make plans to set a fish trap together, a woman begs a bit of yellow dye from a kinswoman, and through the village sounds the rhythmic tattoo which calls the young men together. They gather from all parts of the village, digging sticks in hand, ready to start inland to the plantation. The older men set off upon their more lonely occupations, and each household, reassembled under its peaked roof, settles down to the routine of the morning. Little children, too hungry to wait for the late breakfast, beg lumps of cold taro which they munch greedily. Women carry piles of washing to the sea or to the spring at the far end of the village, or set off inland after weaving materials. The older girls go fishing on the reef, or perhaps set themselves to weaving a new set of Venetian blinds.

In the houses, where the pebbly floors have been swept bare with a stiff long-handled broom, the women great with child and the nursing mothers sit and gossip with one another. Old men sit apart, unceasingly twisting palm husk on their bare thighs and muttering old tales under their breath. The carpenters begin work on the new house, while the owner bustles about trying to keep them in a good humor. Families who will cook today are hard at work; the taro, yams and bananas have already been brought from inland; the children are scuttling back and forth, fetching sea water, or leaves to stuff the pig. As the sun rises higher in the sky, the shadows deepen under the thatched roofs, the sand is burning to the touch, the hibiscus flowers wilt on the hedges, and little children bid the smaller ones, "Come out of the sun." Those whose excursions have been short return to the village, the women with strings of crimson jellyfish, or baskets of shellfish, the men with coconuts, carried in baskets slung on a shoulder pole. The women and children eat their breakfasts, just hot from the oven, if this is cook day, and the young men work swiftly in the midday heat, preparing the noon feast for their elders.

It is high noon. The sand burns the feet of the little children, who leave their palm leaf balls and their pinwheels of frangipani blossoms to wither in the sun, as they creep into the shade of the houses. The women who must go abroad carry great banana leaves as sunshades or wind wet cloths about their heads. Lowering a few blinds against the slanting sun, all who are left in the village wrap their heads in sheets and go to sleep. Only a few adventurous children may slip away for a swim in the shadow of a high rock, some industrious woman continues with her weaving, or a close little group of women bend anxiously over a woman in labor. The village is dazzling and dead; any sound seems oddly loud and out of place. Words have to cut through the solid heat slowly. And then the sun gradually sinks over the sea.

A second time, the sleeping people stir, roused perhaps by the cry of "a boat," resounding through the village. The fishermen beach their canoes, weary and spent from the heat, in spite of the slaked lime on their heads, with which they have sought to cool their brains and redden their hair. The brightly colored fishes are spread out on the floor, or piled in front of the houses until the women pour water over them to free them from taboo. Regretfully, the young fishermen separate out the "Taboo fish," which must be sent to the chief, or proudly they pack the little palm leaf baskets with offerings of fish to take to their sweethearts. Men come home from the bush, grimy and heavy laden, shouting as they come, greeted in a sonorous rising cadence by those who have remained at home. They gather in the guest house for their evening kava drinking. The soft clapping of hands, the high-pitched intoning of the talking chief who serves the kava echoes through the village. Girls gather flowers to weave into necklaces; children, lusty from their naps and bound to no particular task, play circular games in the half shade of the late afternoon. Finally the sun sets, in a flame which stretches from the mountain behind to the horizon on the sea, the last bather comes up from the beach, children straggle home, dark little figures etched against the sky; lights shine in the houses, and each household gathers for its evening meal. The suitor humbly presents his offering, the children have been summoned from their noisy play, perhaps there is an honored guest who must be served first, after the soft, barbaric singing of Christian hymns and the brief and graceful evening prayer. In front of a house at the end of the village, a father cries out the birth of a son. In some family circles a face is missing, in others little runaways have found a haven! Again quiet settles upon the village, as first the head of the household, then the women and children, and last of all the patient boys, eat their supper.

After supper the old people and the little children are bundled off to bed. If the young people have guests the front of the house is yielded to them. For day is the time for the councils of old men and the labors of youth, and night is the time for lighter things. Two kinsmen, or a chief and his councillor, sit and gossip over the day's events or make plans for the morrow. Outside a crier goes through the village announcing that the communal breadfruit pit will be opened in the morning, or that the village will make a great fish trap. If it is moonlight, groups of young men, women by twos and threes, wander through the village, and crowds of children hunt for land crabs or chase each other among the breadfruit trees. Half the village may go fishing by torchlight and the curving reef will gleam with wavering lights and echo with shouts of triumph or disappointment, teasing words or smothered cries of outraged modesty. Or a group of youths may dance for the pleasure of some visiting maiden. Many of those who have retired to sleep, drawn by the merry music, will wrap their sheets about them and set out to find the dancing. A white-clad, ghostly throng will gather in a circle about the gaily lit house, a circle from which every now and then a few will detach themselves and wander away among the trees. Sometimes sleep will not descend upon the village until long past midnight; then at last there is only the mellow thunder of the reef and the whisper of lovers, as the village rests until dawn.

A description of this kind gives an idea of village life, the whole gentle rhythm of life, but it gives no clue to what the anthropologist did on such a day. Later, in 1938, while I was in the field among the Iatmul people of New Guinea, it occurred to me to write a particularly detailed set of entries in my field diary for one day, so that, if ever I wanted to show people what a day in the field was like, I would have this actual record.

On this day we had been in the village of Tambunum, on the Sepik River, for five months. When we first came to the village, we lived at one end of it in a rickety old guest house which the government had required the villagers to build. Arranging to have a house of our own built required dickering and arguing and fussing, first to select a site where the house could be placed and then to get it built. Among the

Iatmul people nothing ever gets done without a great deal of shouting and scolding. People even smash their own property in such arguments, and once, for emphasis, we had to break one of the valuable mother-of-pearl shells we had brought with us, before the villagers would finally finish our house.

Iatmul villages are flooded part of the year, but during the dry season they are high and dry, some twelve feet above the great river. We arrived in Tambunum at the beginning of the dry season and, taking a chance that our fieldwork would be completed before the river water rose, we decided to have our house built on the ground, which could be done more quickly and less expensively. But if our timing was off and the floods came before our work was finished, all our goods would have to be carried up into one of the Iatmul houses. These were built on sturdy posts, with the floor high above ground level. In the dry season the people lived under their houses, using the dry, baked clay as a floor. Fortunately, we did finish before the river rose.

Our house was really two houses, built side by side, each with a high thatched roof. Around the outside was a low fence to keep out the pigs. In the center of each house was a "mosquito room." One of these was a screened box, measuring eight feet on each side, with a screen door. It also had a little pantry window, made of a box with weighted ends, through which food could be pushed. A boy outside would lift one end of the box, put the food in, and close the box; then another boy inside the room would open his end of the box and take the food out. Wire netting was very expensive and even one eight-foot-square room was all we could afford. The other mosquito room was made of sewn copper wire supported by posts. That was where I worked with the women and children. In each house a small corner was walled off, one for a storeroom and the other for a shower room.

For better protection, the bed, too, was tightly covered with a mosquito net. At night you took to bed with you everything you might possibly need; to get up in the middle of the night meant being badly mosquito-bitten. Drinking water, a flashlight to read by, a flit spray, aspirin, a notebook to record bright ideas and shouts and sounds in the nighttime village—all were kept in a small square basket, which we had brought with us from Bali.

The two houses occupied a long piece of land in front of the family houses, between the men's road, which passed along the riverbank, and the women's road farther inland, which passed behind the men's clubhouses. It was an excellent location. While I was sitting at work, I could watch people coming and going and find out, by seeing who was in a group and what their behavior was, whether something was afoot. One reason we picked this site was that Tjamwali (one of the two wives of Baangwin, our neighbor) was soon to have a child, and I hoped to see the birth. In fact, I didn't. The baby was born while Tjamwali was out fishing. But Baangwin's house was so close by that I could hear the slightest sound, and if I heard anything unusual I could jump up, even at night, and go there to see what was happening. Baangwin's brother and his wife lived in the house behind us. Their children's voices, too, could be heard clearly. And on our other side, two houses were well within earshot. Our canoe, with its outboard motor, was moored on the riverbank, and our cookhouse was on the land side, across the women's road.

On the day I recorded particularly carefully, September 18, 1938, we had been installed in our newly built house for two months. The page of my diary on which this account is based had at the top a list of letters that were ready to go whenever the next pinnace (which might belong to a government official, a trader, or a missionary) went past down the river. The letters included orders for supplies, plans for our return to Bali (which had to be made three months in advance), personal letters, information for our income tax, instructions about forwarding mail, a letter to a colleague in the East Indies with whom we were exchanging books, a cable to Jane Belo who was to meet us in Bali, and a short paper written for an anthropological journal. In the field it is important to keep a record of every letter sent and received. When you have your mind on the affairs of a New Guinea village, it is hard to remember what civilization is like. And also, when news is scarce, every bit of news, every new idea or new book, seems terribly important.

In reproducing the notes for that day, I shall use italics for my explanations of and comments on the actual entries. The contrast in the amount of space needed for the entries and for my comments on them gives some idea of the difference between living in the intimacy of village life, where everyone is known and a kind of shorthand can be used to refer to what is happening, and the amount of explanation it takes to make sense of a field trip once you are back home.

The diary runs like this:

5:45—Baangwin started shouting at Purundemi. *Baangwin and Purundemi were clan brothers and were quarreling over the disposal of some crocodile meat.*

Mbetnda took down this quarrel; later was spelled by Tshavi. *I first called my youngest assistant, a fourteen-year-old boy, to dictate to me rapidly what the two men were saying. It is very hard to follow angry idiomatic shouting. It is more efficient to train someone to retell it quickly while the quarrel goes on. When Mbetnda got tired, his place was taken by Tshavi, one of my older informants, who was willing to spend time working with me rather than fishing or working in the bush because he had lost a leg.*

Tshilish went out in a canoe shouting about people who were eating sago. Later in the day this anger proved to have been directed at his sister.

I went through the mail, checked it, signed it.

Observed baby from house 79. Tshuoshavwan and Magiendo—*two other children*—playing. *This meant taking detailed notes.*

Breakfast of fried bananas and coffee with powdered milk.

Baby 79 climbed up on a teva—*mound around a coconut tree*—finally rescued by his grandmother—*paternal.*

Observed Magiendo temper tantrum.

Kanush's son came for medicine. Wound resulted from a blow from his father. Collected the story.

Polipoli came for medicine for abrasion from carrying a bag of betel (*nut*).

Started to type Purundemi quarrel. Manggwa appeared. *One of my best informants.* I realized that I must get the story of last night's return of Aramali's wife while it was fresh. So took dictation of this. Then decided to finish up the old tale of the quarrel between the two wives of Yanagwon, which had never been finished. In the course of this, point came up of giving away kombang—*lime.* Asked if Tomi did this. Manggwa didn't know. Drawing group here. *Groups of children would wander in, ask for paper, kneel anywhere in the house, using tops of boxes as tables, and when they had finished drawing, they would bring the sheets of paper to me to be dated. I would keep track of their comings and goings out of the corner of my eye, while I was taking dictation down on the typewriter.*

While Manggwa was dictating, news came that Karapmi's baby had been born while she was out in the bush. Went over to the house and saw the new baby. Came back and found GB—*my husband*—had just returned from the House Tamberan—*men's house.* We went over and made a film of the mother and new baby.

11:06—Back to room wire—*mosquito room.* Tea.

During tea watched Tjimbindo—*a small child*—playing with an empty cartridge case and Tjimbora handling sleeping Nemangke—*her young daughter.*

Back to more dictation from Manggwa about kombang story.

Procession passed, on the way to give betel to their ceremonial feasting partners in Tavireman—*a small men's house.* Tore after them. Took Mbetnda *as translator* because Tshavi couldn't make pace.

In Tavireman, recorded speeches of Kanyavimali to Yendi Timbunmali. Saw Avitjirai—*co-wife with Karapmi, who had just borne a new baby*—and verified that she knew about the birth and that Komankowi —*the husband*—was away in the bush and didn't know yet.

L (*still photographs with Leica camera*) of Komankowi's baby.

Visited Namwi's baby; L of oldest child showing fear —*of me as stranger*—and of sleeping posture of the baby.

Passed Tergerak's house and discussed his Timbunki visit—*new village up the river*—and found he was ignorant of the abortive Kerambit—*big men's house* —plan to go to Timbki for a second pair of flutes—*used in ceremonial, taboo to women.*

Passed Aramunda, who reported himself ill. I arranged

to take a child back to send him medicine.
Cine (*movie camera record*) and L of Ndamio and Tjimbutondowa.
Passed Kwainye's house. L of sleeping baby 74.
Back to the house, finally finished dictation with Manggwa combined with observations on play with toys—*writing up a set of earlier observations of children playing with a toy snake, doll, and teddy bear.*
12:25—Back to the new baby, Cine and Leica.
Back to house. Tomi there. Asked him about kombang —*ceremonial lime use.*
Lunch.
1:30—Went back to observe new baby again.
Siesta.
3:15—Went to investigate temper tantrum of Kandegwishe, collected Nogwai's account of his betel-nut *ceremony,* and of quarrel between his mother and sister. Recorded Womialyesh's outburst when account of what Tshilish had said about her this morning was reported to her, by Kerremkurtbuangge. Tjimbora—*wife of Baangwin*—began to make a grass skirt, so seized the opportunity to make a detailed account of it with Cine and Leica. Nemangke—*her child*—playing at sago making beside her. Planned to continue this into a film of mother bathing and dressing Nemangke. Tjimbora got out a razor blade to *cut* N's hair. Tjamwali—*Baangwin's other wife, away at home of her own family with her new baby* —arrived to put a taboo on one of Baangwin's coconut palms, and a big quarrel resulted. Followed

quarrel at both ends, with Cine. Swapped Manggwa for Mbetnda—*as informant*—in the middle.
Kwombambwi came to borrow paint—*from us*—for the Tevwa—*funeral figure representing the dead.*
5:00—GB went to the House Tamberan.
Observation of Katali's baby's display of fear.
Puanmangke teasing Getma—*two little girls.*
Eichorn's pinnace arrived.
6:00—Leica of Maleguna's twin in a new grass skirt.
Bath, dinner. Before coffee, news of quarrel between two wives of Vimbli, went down and recorded the plot. Quarrel was over.
GB to Kerambit to check preparations, then back, started cataloguing film.
MM (*myself*) to room wire. Group of children playing with toys. Started typing. Nogwai—*another good informant*—came. Thirty-six hundred words of dictation from Nogwai, myth of men and women, with gestures recorded.
9:45—Diary.
Listing of Cine film.
Bed.

To go back to a diary entry like this one means to wrench one's mind back across the years and across the distance between living in modern America and living in a neolithic world. It takes some time to bring the names into focus, to bring back each person's face, to recall what the quarrels were about. If I had not written the details down at the time, it would be quite impossible to deal with them now. But once the details have been recorded, it is possible to bring them back, especially with photographs and film to help, even a quarter of a century later.

VII

Anthropology as Science and Scholarship, in the Arts and in Planning for Human Welfare

The kind of people who make good anthropologists could have put their abilities to use in many other professions. In the past, a number of anthropologists—Franz Boas, George Bird Grinnell, Ruth Benedict, to name only a few—came into anthropology from other fields. Today more students may come directly into this field. But no single ability or talent is by itself a crucial one.

Although anthropology is a research science, it offers limited opportunities for the "armchair" scholar whose chief area of activities is bounded by library walls. Instead, an anthropologist may spend a great deal of time out-of-doors, living under primitive conditions, very much as an explorer, a prospector, a geologist, or an oil engineer may have to do. Because anthropology means working with people, learning languages is a necessary skill—not merely learning to recognize the written form of another language, as students often do in modern language classes (a kind of learning that may carry them through some other sciences), but learning them as a living form of speech, heard and spoken. Our American methods of teaching often fail a student in this, but the student who decides to be an anthropologist must learn how to learn spoken versions of languages—including those he may be the first to record in written form.

Anthropology takes a lot of hard thinking. But there are many things that have to be done with one's hands—typing notes, sorting and packing and cataloguing specimens, running a tape recorder, taking photographs and developing them. Besides, it is necessary to describe what other people do with their hands—weaving and carving, throwing spears, building houses and canoes, tying knots, making pottery, planting and harvesting crops, cooking and making clothes, fishing and sailing boats. It is difficult to describe accurately all the techniques in which people use their hands unless you are good at using your own and can get a sense of what they are doing.

Above all, anthropology means getting along with

people—not just a few close friends and relatives, but all kinds of people—including the intelligent and the stupid, men and women, the friendly and the bad-tempered, people in high positions and the village ne'er-do-well, sharp traders, the sick and the handicapped as well as healthy people, skilled craftsmen, and dedicated artists. It means having a memory for people and learning to remember who and what they are, in the way that a good politician must, not only recognizing their faces and knowing their names but also keeping in mind details of the things that are important about them. And, almost always, anthropologists need to have a real concern for human beings; they must care about what is happening in their village and tribe and what is happening in the world. An anthropologist who has little feeling for people finds fieldwork too trying and soon gives it up.

Field anthropology involves taking an interest in the arts, having a feeling for the designs people make, the myths they tell, the songs they sing, and their dramatic performances. Very often students are attracted to anthropology through some first acquaintance with an Indian dance, a piece of exotic music, or a collection of folk songs out of our own past. But even those students who are not especially attracted to the arts will find it necessary to know something about them. Not very many will have the kind of talent that Melville Herskovits, for example, had for learning the intricate patterns of African drumming, so that he could play together with the more expert of his informants. But enough interest and ability to understand is necessary so that talking with an expert is enjoyable to both of them. Of course, students who are already interested in the arts will have to make a choice among the various ones in which anthropologists specialize in order to develop this interest into a first-rate skill.

Anthropologists also must understand and care about good scholarship. They must know how to work with old documents, unpublished government reports, musty, crumbling records of old explorations, diaries and surveyors' maps, tax records, parish records and local censuses, and missionaries' accounts of the "cruel and barbarous behavior" of the people they came to convert. It may be necessary, for research purposes, to learn an archaic form of a language—medieval Latin or Old Icelandic. Or it may be necessary to classify records written in Spanish describing the Southwest before this region became part of the United States. Or research may combine a study of nineteenth-century New England tombstones with an analysis of the records of the religious thought of the period, as in a project James Deetz of the University of California at Santa Barbara has been working on.

Clearly, while anthropologists cannot be "armchair" scholars, they also cannot be the kind of people (as some journalists and psychiatrists are) who only enjoy working with people and find work with books a deadly bore. Essentially, anthropologists are people who enjoy the discovery of living culture in all its diversity, whether research takes the form of discovery of the distant past, through the evidence of the bones of very early men, or a find of flaked-stone tools, or the crumbling outlines of an ancient, long-buried city; whether an old culture emerges from an investigation into the early forms of government in Iceland through a search of old records and traditional tales or from a study of the correspondence and records and orders of fur trading companies in their relations with the Indians to whom they sold guns and traps; or whether research takes the multiple forms of modern fieldwork. On the balance, an anthropologist will develop most fully the skills he needs to work on the problems and the areas of his special choice. But what holds anthropologists together is their common interest in living cultures, old and new.

Some of their ways of thinking and working tie them very closely to the natural sciences. Anthropologists must understand how to approach a problem scientifically, that is, how to establish hypotheses that can be tested, retested, and revised in the light of new evidence. For their work they need to draw now on one natural science and now on another—geology, botany, physiology, anatomy, ornithology, physics, and chemistry. One cannot always predict which body of scientific information it will be necessary to tap for the solution of some problem. The archeologist digging in a kitchen midden (an ancient rubbish heap) and the ethnologist working with the modern people whose village is built close by, perhaps even on top of, the archeologist's site, may try to establish a link between past and present through an analysis of food particles or a combined analysis of old pottery sherds and modern pottery-making techniques. Whatever their problem, anthropologists must understand science as a way of thinking and carrying out investigations, and they must know enough about other sciences both to ask meaningful questions and to make use of the information other scientists can supply.

When I was in college, it seemed to me that I could make one of three choices: I could be a scientist or an artist or I could go into politics and try to improve the state of the world right away. I looked over my assets. I had done enough painting to have reason to think I *might* become a painter. I was interested in writing and had enough talent so it was reasonable to think I *might* become a writer. I could talk in public, something I had found out during World War I, when I made four-minute speeches to persuade people to buy war savings stamps.

My father was an economist who was interested in the operation of real companies in the actual business world. My mother was a sociologist who had studied an Italian immigrant community. My grandmother was an educator who was interested in new theories of education—the Montessori method of teaching, what we now call "the new mathematics," and all the stages of children's learning. Social science was something I was accustomed to think about. So was social welfare, for my mother was passionately interested in problems of righting social wrongs—eliminating slums and sweatshops, improving the conditions of life of members of other races, and advancing the rights of women. And in those days, when there was less clarity about the nature of fieldwork, scientific work and scholarly work seemed to me to be all of one piece.

It was hard to make a choice. There were so many fascinating things to do, on any one of which one could spend a lifetime. A life did not then stretch ahead as far as it does now. But our picture of the future was as yet not shadowed by the threat that our failure to preserve peace might end human living altogether.

Finally, I decided on science. For in science every contribution, however small and uninspired and routine it may be, still counts. The arts, in 1923—and, indeed, the arts today—are fields in which one must excel if one's contribution is to matter. There are very few places in the contemporary world that resemble the great painters' studios in Renaissance Florence, where the less gifted artist spent his time painting angels' wings while the more gifted artist painted the angels' faces.

I chose science because I wanted to be sure that my work would count. And I turned to the social sciences because my interests lie in what happens to people. But the actual choice was still unclear. In testing psychology, for example, there seemed to be little room for speech-making or even writing.

As a senior at Barnard College, I started to study

anthropology—and two things happened at the same time. I discovered in Professor Franz Boas the greatest mind I had ever encountered and I discovered in anthropology a fascinating field in which my several interests—in people, in science, in the fate of human beings, in the arts, in writing, and in speaking—could be combined. I lay awake all one night. By morning I had decided to become an anthropologist.

No two students are confronted with the same set of opportunities. The greatest mind that a student may encounter may be in a field other than the one which he is thinking of making his own. But it is entirely worth the effort of taking some work with him or her just to get the feel of someone with full mastery of a subject. And all students have their own particular sets of choices to reconcile.

Anthropology opens the door to a wide range of choices.* A student may be interested in music, for example. Today there is a whole new field of comparative analysis of music, developed by Alan Lomax, called cantometrics. Or a musician may hope to combine composing with the study of some non-European musical tradition, as Colin McPhee did in his lifetime work on the music of Bali. New specialties are continually springing up. One of these is kinesics, the study of nonverbal behavior and the patterning of gesture. Another, semiotics, considers all forms of

* The reading list at the end of the book gives a sampling of what some of these choices are.

communication, verbal and nonverbal, grouped together.

A student may be interested in film-making. Today it is possible to become an anthropological film-maker. This generation's film-makers will make the last precious filmed records of primitive peoples; but successive films, recording change, are beginning to provide new sources for study. Another student may be fascinated by the problems of history and plan to combine studies of living peoples with research on their past, over long stretches of time.

Applied anthropology, in which our knowledge of human cultures and especially the methods of work that have been developed are brought to bear on practical problems, is continually opening new areas. In this field anthropology combines with mental-health research, nutrition, town planning, international communication, automation, public health, and education in our own country and in nations that are struggling with the problems of coming into the modern world. Applied anthropologists, among others, have helped in the training of the Peace Corps and, in turn, people who have worked in the Peace Corps may well contribute to thinking in applied anthropology.

Anthropology has to do with man as a physical as well as a social and a thinking being. Physical anthropology also has greatly expanded in recent years. There are anthropologists who go to the field to study primate societies in their natural habitat—gorillas, chimpanzees, baboons, langurs, and others. In Japan, a research station has been established to study colonies of Japanese monkeys living under various conditions, partly as a way of understanding better how new kinds of learning take place and spread through a group. All these studies give us a wider background for understanding man. Other anthropologists are studying the distribution of blood types in human populations and the relationship of these distributions to such things as changes in nutrition and human migration.

Today, especially, it is important to understand how mankind spread over the face of the earth and why, in our species, Homo sapiens, whose members have the same original range and kinds of ability, some peoples at particular periods in human history have leaped ahead while others have kept to old traditional ways of life. It is important for us to understand what it means for a people to be in the main current of history or, on the contrary, for a people to be isolated from that mainstream, cut off from the conditions and the events that lead to change and new inventions. It is important for us, also, to understand what it means to live as a full member of a settled group and at the center of things or, on the contrary, to be part of a migrating group, entering another country under conditions of disadvantage, poverty, and (as happens very commonly today) heavy work, such as mining or crop-picking, which other people disdain to do.

In the world in which we live, one question of the greatest importance is that of evolution, both the evolution of life on our planet, in our solar system, and in our Galaxy, and the evolution of man to his present highly responsible place among all living creatures. Great biologists (Julian Huxley, for example) and scientists who are profoundly religious men (Père Teilhard de Chardin, for example, the French prehistorian who worked in China for many years on the problems of early man) are equally concerned with the direction in which mankind is moving now that life on our planet has become closely interconnected and we have actually begun to explore the universe.

The role human beings, using science, can play in assuring the safety of mankind and in constructing human societies closer to men's hearts' desires is a question the urgency of which will not decrease perhaps for centuries to come. It may be that students now planning for their future careers will, in their lifetime, be able to take a hand in the construction of the first space colonies. Before this can be accomplished it will be necessary to ask—and answer—new questions about human capabilities, human potentialities, and human limitations. And it will be necessary to work out, in these terms, the size, the density, and the range of population for a completely preselected group of space colonists.

Looking ahead, it may well be that the tiny island societies of the South Seas—many of them isolated from one another for centuries and all of them isolated from the rest of the world until they were visited by explorers and missionaries and traders and were studied by anthropologists like myself, as I went out on my early field trips—will provide us with living models for two new kinds of islands.

The first of these new islands is the earth itself. The second will be the kind of satellite on which we may, very soon, establish our first colonies in the wider universe. A space colony may have, over a long period of time, no communication with other men. It will be a little world, free to solve its own problems, fight its only enemies—hunger, disease, and disorder—and make its own new inventions. And it will be lonely, not on the uncharted oceans of the world but in the new isolation of space.

Anthropology is a discipline in which a student can bring into play every gift, every interest, and every skill; a discipline which allows him to live as a whole human being while he makes his best contribution to the future of man.

Appendix A

Information for a Career in Anthropology

Preparing for college

The student who plans to do any work in anthropology will need a master's degree (M.A.) in anthropology; for most professional work a doctoral degree (Ph.D.) also will be necessary. The student who is already interested in anthropology in high school can choose a college with a strong anthropology department. Usually this means doing undergraduate work in a university with a good graduate department of anthropology.

For information about requirements and a general

overview of the field, you can send for the valuable little booklet by William C. Sturtevant, *Anthropology as a Career*. (Address your request to the Bureau of American Ethnology, Smithsonian Institution, Washington, D.C. 2000.) This pamphlet contains many good suggestions. For instance, Sturtevant points out that many things you may think of as irrelevant—things you may have learned how to do in scouting or in school clubs, such as weaving, or photography, or efficient camping techniques—may be useful assets.

For college information

To find out which colleges teach anthropology, you may ask your school adviser to look up for you the colleges that are not affiliated with larger institutions. Then, for universities where you can begin undergraduate work in anthropology, there is another resource. Locate a current issue of the *American Anthropologist*, the journal of the American Anthropological Association. Inside the front cover you will find (listed under "Information for Subscribers") the Association's current address. By writing to the American Anthropological Association at this address, you can obtain an annual *Guide to Graduate Departments of Anthropology*.

Conditions change very rapidly. New departments are organized, and other departments, where sociology (or perhaps social psychology or human geography) has been grouped with anthropology, may subdivide. In any case, information goes quickly out of date. So you must keep yourself currently informed.

At college: special skills and languages

While you are an undergraduate student, you will do well to acquire a sound grounding in the biological sciences, the best training you can get in good, straightforward writing, and a knowledge of at least two foreign languages. French and German are the basic ones usually required for a Ph.D. But a student who knows that he or she is interested in a particular area of the world often may substitute such languages as Russian, Chinese, Spanish, Portuguese, Japanese, Hindi, or Urdu.

Basic skills, such as still and movie photography, the management of a tape recorder, touch-typing, stenography, speedwriting, or stenotyping, all should be acquired during the undergraduate years. If it is possible to do so, you should get some preliminary training in archeological skills and in linguistics as well. With these things well in hand, you will come to graduate school free to work rapidly toward fieldwork and a graduate degree.

Opportunities for work

A student who attends a college with a long winter vacation (Antioch, Bennington, and others) or a school which has adopted the quarterly or the trimester system (this includes many state universities) has the opportunity to look for work experience during the winter months, a time when most anthropologists are home from the field to teach and work on their field materials.

Summer field trips for students are sponsored by

individual colleges and universities or sometimes by a cluster of institutions (as, for example, a joint program which was sponsored by four universities in the early 1960's). In deciding on a college, it is useful to find out whether it has an ongoing program of summer fieldwork in which undergraduate students can participate.

Other places where you may be able to get work experience or training are museums and laboratories that are near your college or are accessible to you in the summertime. The Smithsonian Institution in Washington, D.C. is a good starting point if you are lacking in local resources. Occasionally, the Smithsonian Institution may have openings for qualified students in one of its departments, at the United States National Museum, or on archeological digs, which may be related to salvage archeology programs. You may write to the Smithsonian Institution for advice and information.

A student who knows about ongoing programs of government assistance for undergraduate research training may find it helpful to mention such possibilities in a letter of application to a museum. Sometimes this will stimulate a local museum to apply for such assistance.

In applying for a vacation job, whether it is paid or voluntary, or for a place in a field-trip program, make the most of your assets. But be realistic with yourself and with others about what your current qualifications are.

Opportunities for scholarships and fellowships

Because of the rapidity with which conditions change, it is possible only to give general rather than specific advice. As early as possible, you should begin to check to find out which government agencies and foundations are currently offering scholarships for undergraduates, either for the school year or for summer research or training.

You must apply for scholarships for study as well as for summer work well in advance. If you are looking for an opportunity for summer work at the end of your junior year in college, for example, you should start making inquiries at the end of your sophomore year, so you can get your applications to the proper offices by early autumn of your junior year. Students lose many good opportunities by waiting too long to explore the possibilities.

College seniors, in particular, should look into the possibility of obtaining a Woodrow Wilson fellowship (particularly for first-year graduate work). Grants for graduate fellowships can be sought from government agencies, particularly the National Institutes of Health and the National Science Foundation. Other types of fellowship programs are under the auspices of the National Research Council, the Social Science Research Council, and the American Council of Learned Societies. Some awards are based on special competitive examinations.

Graduate fellowships take longer to process than those for undergraduates. Requests for field grants take even longer, because purchases must be approved before the administrative work can begin, and many pieces of necessary equipment may take weeks or even months to obtain. Again, you must start early.

You should also be alert to the ways in which programs of wider scope (such as the language fellowships under the National Defense Education Act) may be relevant to your special abilities and needs.

The large foundations have a variety of programs into which anthropology sometimes fits. In addition, there are smaller foundations with special interests in areas or in subject matter that are directly relevant.

One organization specifically devoted to anthropology is the Wenner-Gren Foundation for Anthropological Research, located at 14 East 71 Street, New York 10021. Among the societies having area interests are the Asia Society, the Far East Association, the Iranian Institute, the Andean Society, and the Institute for Intercultural Studies. But there are many others. You should apply to them for information about special opportunities.

Still other organizations are interested in the needs of particular types of students. The American Association of University Women gives fellowships to women students for graduate and for postgraduate research. The Whitney Foundation is interested in the career development of members of ethnic minorities. There are also special programs for individuals with sensory handicaps. Careful exploration of these several opportunities is one good way of beginning a research career.

The two basic handbooks in your search for grants are *Fellowships in the Arts and Sciences,* edited by Robert Quick (American Council on Education, 1785 Massachusetts Avenue, N.W., Washington, D.C. 2000) and *The Foundation Directory,* edited by Ann D. Walton and F. Emerson Andrews (Russell Sage Foundation, 230 Park Avenue, New York 10017).

Starting out

For many readers, discussions of graduate fellowships and travel grants don't yet apply. They are at a distance, still, from college. If you are one of these readers, the descriptions of scholarships and fellowships and summer training programs are intended to show you that the way ahead is open—when you are ready.

But you can be thinking about summer experience, perhaps even volunteer work in a local archeological project or museum. Or through your local museum or a nearby college, you may find an anthropologist or archeologist who can use your skills and, in return, will help you learn more about anthropology.

The first requisites for getting and holding jobs like these are good fast typing, skills like handling film and prints carefully, and, above all, high-level accuracy. In anthropology we often are handling objects that are unique and priceless. Care and accuracy are essential. Doing a job of this kind is like parachute jumping —you have to get it right the first time.

Appendix B

Biographical Sketches

Conrad M. Arensberg was born in Pittsburgh, Pennsylvania, on September 12, 1910. He studied at Harvard University, where he received his B.A. degree in 1931 and his Ph.D. degree in 1934. At present he is Professor of Anthropology at Columbia University.

Dr. Arensberg is a social anthropologist who has a special interest in research on the community: defining what a community is, examining contemporary settlements in terms of what they retain from the past and how they respond to the impact of change, and comparing different forms of community. He is interested also in industrial organization, applied anthropology, and problems of culture change in Europe, the Middle East, and India. The scope of his interests is reflected in his fieldwork, which includes a study of an Irish village, research on modern American communities, and, more recently, work in India.

Interview, pp. 85–87.

JUNIUS B. BIRD was born in Rye, New York, on September 21, 1907. In 1927, he left his studies at Columbia University to go to Baffin Island in the Arctic, on his first archeological expedition. He has an honorary D.Sc. degree from Wesleyan University, and in 1957 he was awarded the Viking Fund Medal for outstanding work in archeology. He is Curator of South American Archeology at The American Museum of Natural History.

His fieldwork ranges the Americas from the Arctic in the north to Tierra del Fuego at the southernmost tip of South America. His interests range widely also in American archeology and problems of the early migration of man in the New World. In the course of his field research he discovered important evidence on the ancient presence of man in South America. A specialist on prehistoric fabrics in South America, he has recently extended his encyclopedic knowledge of the subject to the study of fabric impress on early pottery from Afghanistan, Pakistan, and India.

Interview, pp. 23–32.

RUTH L. BUNZEL was born in New York City on

April 18, 1898. A graduate of Barnard College, she entered anthropology by way of secretarial work for Professor Franz Boas, and received her Ph.D. from Columbia University in 1929. She is now Adjunct Professor of Anthropology at Columbia University.

Dr. Bunzel, a cultural anthropologist, was a pioneer in the study of individuality among North American Indians. Her principal fieldwork was done among the Zuni and in the Guatemalan highlands. She has published monographs on Zuni grammar, Zuni religious life, and the texts of their myths, as well as *Pueblo Potter* (1929), a classic study of the relation of the artist to her work, and *Chichicastenango* (1952), a study of a Guatemalan village. Her present interest is mainly in modern cultures, particularly China and the United States.

Interview, pp. 87–91.

Robert L. Carneiro was born in New York City on June 4, 1927. He studied at the University of Michigan, where he received his B.A. in 1949 and his Ph.D. in 1957. He is Associate Curator of South American Ethnology at The American Museum of Natural History.

A specialist in the field of South American Indian studies, Dr. Carneiro is particularly interested in ecology—the relation of man to his environment—and in the history of man's social development. Together with his anthropologist wife, Dr. Gertrude E. Dole, he has made field trips to the Kuikuru Indians in central

Brazil and to the Amahuaca Indians of eastern Peru.
Interview, pp. 32–41.

HAROLD C. CONKLIN was born on April 27, 1926, in Easton, Pennsylvania. He did his undergraduate work at the University of California at Berkeley, and received his Ph.D. from Yale University in 1955. Formerly at Columbia University, he is now Chairman of the Department of Anthropology at Yale University.

Dr. Conklin has been interested all his professional life in man's relation to his natural environment. Trained as a linguist, he combines linguistic analysis with detailed studies of ecology. His main research area is Southeast Asia, particularly the Philippine Islands, where he has done intensive fieldwork.
Interview, pp. 91–93.

GERTRUDE E. DOLE was born in Cavendish, Vermont, on October 10, 1915. She received her B.A. from Middlebury College, Vermont, where she specialized in Biology and French. Later she did graduate work at the University of North Carolina and received her Ph.D. in anthropology from the University of Michigan in 1957. At present she teaches in the Department of Sociology and Anthropology at New York University.

Dr. Dole's principal interest is in problems of social organization, particularly the development of kinship. She has done fieldwork in Brazil and in eastern Peru together with her anthropologist husband, Robert L.

Carneiro, and works closely with him in his research at the Museum.

Interview, pp. 32–41.

Gordon F. Ekholm was born in St. Paul, Minnesota, on November 25, 1909. After completing his undergraduate studies at the University of Minnesota in 1933, he went to Harvard University for his graduate work and received his Ph.D. in 1941. Dr. Ekholm is Curator of Mexican Archeology at The American Museum of Natural History.

His major research area has been Mexico and Central America, where he has done extensive fieldwork. An expert on pre-Columbian art, he has recently become interested in the problems of transpacific contacts in the New World, as he has traced parallels to art styles of the New World.

Interview, pp. 46–51.

Walter A. Fairservis, Jr., was born on February 17, 1921, in Brooklyn, New York. After receiving his B.A. in 1943 and his M.A. in 1949 from Columbia University, he went to Harvard University, where he received a second M.A. in 1951 and his Ph.D. in 1958. Formerly a Research Associate at The American Museum of Natural History, Dr. Fairservis is now Director of the Thomas Burke Memorial Washington State Museum at the University of Washington in Seattle.

Dr. Fairservis is an archeologist whose central interest is in the early civilizations of the Middle East, from Egypt to India. He saw something of China during World War II, and archeological fieldwork has taken him to Afghanistan, Pakistan, and India.

Interview, pp. 41–46.

STANLEY A. FREED was born in Springfield, Ohio, on April 18, 1927. He did undergraduate work at Ohio State University and the University of Chicago, where he obtained a Ph.B. degree. In 1957, he received his Ph.D. from the University of California at Berkeley. He is Assistant Curator of North American Ethnology at The American Museum of Natural History.

Dr. Freed's interest in ethnology, especially in problems of social organization, has led to work both with North American Indians and with the cultures of India. Two field trips in the United States took him to the Washo of western Nevada and eastern California, and the Mohave of southern California. Later, working with his anthropologist wife, Dr. Ruth Freed, he made an intensive study in India of the effects of city living on the lives of villagers who moved from country to city.

Interview, pp. 51–57.

MORTON H. FRIED was born in New York City on March 21, 1923. After graduating from the College of the City of New York in 1942, he did special work on the Far East and studied Chinese at Harvard University; in 1955 he received his Ph.D. from Columbia University. He is now Professor of Anthropology at Columbia University.

Dr. Fried, a cultural anthropologist, has a wide

range of interests, including social and political organization and problems of cultural evolution. One of a handful of modern ethnologists who have done fieldwork on Chinese culture, Dr. Fried spent almost a year and a half, in the late 1940's, studying the town of Ch'uhsien, not far from Nanking. He has also studied overseas Chinese, in the Caribbean area and elsewhere, and he recently made a year's study of the Chinese of Taiwan, whose forebears many generations ago migrated to the island from mainland China.

Interview, pp. 94–97.

Philip C. Gifford was born in Providence, Rhode Island, on October 28, 1919. He did his undergraduate work in sociology at Haverford College, where he received his B.S. in 1941. In 1949 he received a degree in industrial design from the Rhode Island School of Design, and in 1953 his M.A. in anthropology from Columbia University. One of his special interests has been jewelry design. At The American Museum of Natural History, he is in charge of the Museum's vast collections of anthropological materials. Mr. Gifford's present research interest is in the relation of art style to culture, particularly in the South Pacific area.

Interview, pp. 62–72.

Joseph H. Greenberg was born in Brooklyn, New York, on May 28, 1915. He did his undergraduate work at Columbia University, and received his Ph.D. from Northwestern University in 1940. A former member of the Department of Anthropology at Columbia University, he is now Professor of Anthropology at Stanford University in California.

Dr. Greenberg is a linguist who has specialized in the languages of Africa (of which there are some 800); he has also done fieldwork in Africa. He has a special interest also in the general theory of language, including universal aspects of language.

Interview, pp. 97–101.

JOAN P. MENCHER was born in New York City on January 29, 1930. After completing her undergraduate work at Smith College in 1950, she did graduate work at Columbia University and received her Ph.D. in 1958. Her first research (on which she wrote her doctoral dissertation) was on family life among Puerto Ricans living in New York City. But her major research area is India, where she has made two extended field trips to study family roles and relationships among the people of South Malabar.

In 1961–62, Dr. Mencher held an Ogden Mills Fellowship at The American Museum of Natural History, which allowed her to do research connected with her fieldwork interests. She is now with the Department of Anthropology at Cornell University.

Interview, pp. 58–62.

HARRY L. SHAPIRO was born in Boston, Massachusetts, on March 19, 1902. After graduating magna cum laude from Harvard College in 1923, he went on to graduate work and received his Ph.D. from Harvard University in 1926. He is Chairman of the Department of Anthropology at The American Museum of Natural History.

Dr. Shapiro, who is a physical anthropologist, began his field research at the age of twenty-one with a trip to Norfolk Island (a tiny island about 900 miles north of Sydney, Australia). There and, in the mid-1930's, on Pitcairn Island (a still smaller Polynesian island), he made a genetic study of the descendants of a small group of Polynesian women and the mutineers of the British ship *Bounty,* who settled on Pitcairn in 1790.

Dr. Shapiro's research interests range widely in ethnology as well as in physical anthropology. One special interest is in the physical effects of migration on human populations. He took part in an archeological expedition to the Marquesas Islands and, in 1948, directed the Joint Biological and Cultural Survey of Puerto Rico. Various research interests have also taken him to Quebec, Alaska, Hawaii, Tahiti, Japan, and China.

Interview, pp. 72–78.

Ralph S. Solecki was born in Brooklyn, New York, on October 15, 1917. He did his undergraduate work at the College of the City of New York, and received his M.A. degree in 1949 and his Ph.D. degree in 1958 from Columbia University. He is Associate Professor of Anthropology at Columbia University.

Dr. Solecki, who is an archeologist, is primarily interested in prehistory and in the problems of the migrations of early man. As part of his field research, he has explored northern Alaska for traces of man's early migrations from Asia into the New World. Other field research has taken him to the Middle East, to Iraq, where he took part in the work that led to the discovery, in Shanidar Cave, of very significant finds of Neanderthal remains. He has also had a part in the archeological rescue operations in the area of Egypt to be flooded by the waters of the great Aswân Dam.

Interview, pp. 102–106.

WILLIAM DUNCAN STRONG was born in Portland, Oregon, on January 30, 1899. He died in Kent Cliffs, New York, on January 29, 1962. He did both his undergraduate and his graduate work at the University of California at Berkeley and received his Ph.D. in 1926. Dr. Strong taught anthropology at Columbia University for over twenty years. He served as Chairman of the Department and also, as Loubat Professor, occupied an endowed chair in Meso-American archeology. Earlier in his career, as well as during World War II, he was attached to the Bureau of American Ethnology, Smithsonian Institution, Washington, D.C.

His principal interest was in the development of cultures, from ancient times, in the New World, including both North and South America, and he pioneered in combining archeological and ethnological methods in the study of culture over time. His field research ranged widely from Naskapi Indian settlements in Labrador, to the Indians of the Great Plains in the United States, south to Central America, and to South America, particularly Peru.

Interview, pp. 106–110.

Colin M. Turnbull was born in Harrow, Middlesex, England, on November 23, 1924. He studied at Oxford, where he received his B.A., M.A., and B.Litt. degrees and, in 1963, his D.Phil. in social anthropology. He also studied in the School of Oriental and African Studies, University of London, and had a research fellowship in the Department of Indian Philosophy at the University of Benares in India. He is Assistant Curator of African Ethnology at The American Museum of Natural History.

Dr. Turnbull's major field research in Africa has been with the Pygmies of the Ituri Forest, about whom he wrote *The Forest People* (1962). He is interested in problems of tribalism, especially as the new problems of nationhood are affecting every aspect of life in the new countries of Africa. An accomplished musician, he has a special interest in primitive music.

Interview, pp. 19–22.

Charles Wagley was born in Clarksville, Texas, on November 9, 1913. He began his undergraduate work at the University of Oklahoma but completed it at Columbia University in 1936, where he also received his Ph.D. in 1941. He is Professor of Anthropology at Columbia University and Director of the Columbia University Institute of Latin American Studies.

Dr. Wagley has done field research in Guatemala and in Brazil, including a study of the Tapirapé Indians. He has also lived and worked in Rio de Janeiro, where he formed close ties with his Brazilian colleagues. He is a social anthropologist who is interested in social organization and social change, race relations, and the problems of ethnic minorities, and, over a long period, the complexities of inter-American relations and the role of anthropology in bringing about a better understanding among peoples of different cultures.

Interview, pp. 110–113.

Books for Further Reading

This list is intended to help you find your way further into anthropology—to find out more about what anthropologists do and how they go about their work. Three kinds of books are included in this list:

1. *Books which are basic in anthropology and books which will give you a general picture of some branches of this science.* Clyde Kluckhohn's *Mirror for Man* and Ralph Linton's *The Tree of Culture* are both intended for readers who are finding out what anthropology is about.
2. *Books which are intended for younger beginners.* All these are listed with one star (*Allen, Agnes. *The Story of Anthropology*). These are books you may enjoy reading aloud to a younger brother or sister. Ralph and Adelin Linton's *Man's Way from Cave to Skyscraper* makes a good beginning.

3. *Books which are more difficult and some on special subjects.* All these are listed with two stars (**Belo, Jane. *Trance in Bali*). These books also sample some of the newer fields, where anthropology touches on other sciences, especially those mentioned in Chapter VII.

Most books are listed first in their original editions. This will tell you when a book was written—whether it represents anthropological thinking in the 1920's or in very recent years. It will also help you find books in your library catalogue. A few books (for instance, Colin McPhee's *House in Bali*) are out of print. You will not be able to buy them, but they can be found in libraries.

Paperback editions, most of which are inexpensive, also are listed. These are given with the name of the paperback publisher and, usually, with a series number (for example, for Ruth Benedict's *Patterns of Culture,* "New York: New American Library, 1946 (MD89)"—with the series number last). New paperbacks are being published every week, and some books appear in several series. If you cannot buy the books you would like in your bookstore, you can order them from the publisher. The New American Library of World Literature (P.O. Box 2310, Grand Central Station, New York, N.Y., 10017) has published *A Guide to Science Reading,* ed. Hilary J. Deason. This book, which was prepared especially for students by the American Association for the Advancement of Science, will give you further leads. It also lists (pp. 191–94) the names and addresses of a great many paperback publishers. Or your bookstore may help you find books in *Paperbound Books in Print,* a cumulative index published periodically by the R. R. Bowker Company.

*Allen, Agnes. *The Story of Archeology.* New York: Philosophical Library, 1958.

**Bateson, Gregory, and Margaret Mead. *Balinese Character: A Photographic Analysis.* Special Publications of The New York Academy of Sciences, 2. New York, 1942. Reprinted 1962.

**Belo, Jane. *Trance in Bali.* New York: Columbia University Press, 1960.

Benedict, Ruth. *Patterns of Culture.* Boston: Houghton Mifflin, 1934. New York: New American Library, 1946 (MD89). Paperback.

**Birdwhistell, Ray L. "The Kinesic Level in the Investigation of the Emotions." In *Expression of the Emotions in Man,* ed. Peter H. Knapp. New York: International Universities Press, 1963, pp. 123–39.

Blowsnake, Sam. *Autobiography of a Winnebago Indian,* by Paul Radin. New York: Dover, 1960. Paperback. First published 1920 under the title *Crashing Thunder: The Autobiography of an American Indian.*

**Boas, Franz. *Primitive Art.* Oslo, 1927. New York: Dover, 1955 (T25). Paperback.

———. *Anthropology and Modern Life.* New York: Norton, 1928. New York: Norton, 1962 (N108). Paperback.

Bohannan, Paul. *Africa and Africans.* American Museum Science Books. Garden City, N. Y.: Natural History Press, 1964 (B8). Paperback.

Braidwood, Robert J. *Archeologists and What They Do.* New York: Watts, 1960.

Casagrande, Joseph B., ed. *In the Company of Man: Twenty Portraits by Anthropologists.* New York: Harper, 1960. New York: Harper and Row, 1964 (TB/3047). Paperback.

**Chapple, Eliot D., and Leonard R. Sayles. *The Measure of Management.* New York: Macmillan, 1961.

Childe, V. Gordon. *Man Makes Himself.* London: Watts, 1936.

New York: New American Library, 1951 (M64). Paperback.

Clark, W. E. Le Gros. *History of the Primates,* rev. ed. Chicago: University of Chicago Press, 1957 (P21). Paperback.

Coon, Carleton A. *The Story of Man.* New York: Knopf, 1954.

Covarrubias, Miguel. *Island of Bali.* New York: Knopf, 1937.

Drucker, Philip. *Indians of the Northwest Coast.* New York: McGraw-Hill, 1955. American Museum Science Books, Garden City, N. Y.: Natural History Press, 1963 (B3). Paperback.

Dunn, L. C., and Th. Dobzhansky. *Heredity, Race, and Society,* rev. ed. New York: New American Library, 1952 (MD74). Paperback.

*Edel, May. *Story of People.* Boston: Little, Brown, 1953.

———. *The Story of Our Ancestors.* Boston: Little, Brown, 1955.

Eiseley, Loren. *The Immense Journey.* New York: Random House, 1957 (Modern Library P47). Paperback.

**Erasmus, Charles J. *Man Takes Control.* Minneapolis: University of Minnesota Press, 1961.

**Erikson, Erik H. *Childhood and Society.* New York: Norton, 1950. Rev. ed., 1964. Paperback.

Frazer, Sir James G. *The Golden Bough: A Study in Magic and Religion,* abridged ed. New York: Macmillan, 1922. New York: Macmillan, 1960 (MP5). Paperback.

**Friedl, Ernestine. *Vasilika: A Village in Modern Greece.* New York: Holt, Rinehart and Winston, 1962. Paperback.

**Goffman, Erving. *Presentation of Self in Everyday Life.* New York: Doubleday, 1959 (A174). Paperback.

Hawkes, Jacquetta, and Christopher Hawkes. *Prehistoric Britain.* Baltimore: Penguin Books, 1958 (Pelican A115). Paperback.

**Huxley, Julian S., ed. *The Humanist Frame.* New York: Harper, 1962.

**Keesing, Felix M. *Native Peoples of the Pacific World.* New York: Macmillan, 1954.

Klineberg, Otto. *Race and Psychology.* Paris: Unesco, 1958. Distributed by Columbia University Press, New York: Paperback.

Kluckhohn, Clyde. *Mirror for Man: The Relation of Anthropology to Modern Life.* New York: Whittlesey House, McGraw-Hill, 1949. Greenwich, Conn.: Fawcett, 1957 (D58). Paperback.

Kroeber, Theodora. *Ishi in Two Worlds: A Biography of the Last Wild Indian in North America.* Berkeley and Los Angeles: University of California Press, 1961. Paperback edition, University of California Press, 1964.

*Laird, Helene, and Charlton Laird. *The Tree of Language.* Cleveland and New York: World Publishing, 1957.

Lee, Dorothy. *Freedom and Culture.* Englewood Cliffs, N. J.: Prentice-Hall, 1959 (S-6). Paperback.

Lewis, Oscar. *Tepoztlan: Village in Mexico.* New York: Holt, Rinehart and Winston, 1960. Paperback.

**———. *The Children of Sanchez.* New York: Random House, 1961. New York: Random House, 1963 (VG-1). Paperback.

Linton, Ralph. *The Tree of Culture.* New York: Knopf, 1956. New York: Random House, 1958 (V76). Paperback.

*———, and Adelin Linton. *Man's Way from Cave to Skyscraper.* New York: Harper, 1947.

Lowie, Robert H. *Indians of the Plains.* New York: McGraw-Hill, 1954. American Museum Science Books. Garden City, N. Y.: Natural History Press, 1964 (B8). Paperback.

Macgowan, Kenneth, and Joseph A. Hester, Jr. *Early Man in*

the New World, rev. ed. Natural History Library. Garden City, N. Y.: Doubleday, 1962 (N22). Paperback.

McPhee, Colin. *A House in Bali.* New York: Day, 1946.

**———. "Children and Music in Bali," in *Childhood in Contemporary Cultures,* Margaret Mead and Martha Wolfenstein, eds. Chicago: University of Chicago Press, 1955, pp. 70–94. Chicago: University of Chicago Press, 1963 (P124). Paperback.

**Malinowski, Bronislaw. *Argonauts of the Western Pacific.* London: Routledge, 1922. New York: Dutton, 1962 (D74). Paperback.

Mead, Margaret, and Ruth L. Bunzel, eds. *The Golden Age of American Anthropology.* New York: Braziller, 1960.

**Mead, Margaret, and Martha Wolfenstein, eds. *Childhood in Contemporary Cultures.* Chicago: University of Chicago Press, 1955. Chicago: University of Chicago Press, 1963 (P124). Paperback.

*Oakley, Kenneth P. *Man the Tool-Maker.* Chicago: University of Chicago Press, 1957 (P20). Paperback.

Oliver, Douglas L. *Invitation to Anthropology.* American Museum Science Books. Garden City, N. Y.: Natural History Press, 1964 (B5). Paperback.

**Paul, Benjamin D., ed. *Health, Culture and Community.* New York: Russell Sage Foundation, 1955. Paperback edition, Russell Sage Foundation, 1964.

Pei, Mario. *The Story of Language.* Philadelphia: Lippincott, 1949. New York: New American Library, 1960 (MQ492). Paperback.

**Pitt-Rivers, Julian A. *People of the Sierra.* New York: Criterion, 1954. Chicago: University of Chicago Press, 1961 (P55). Paperback.

Redfield, Robert. *The Primitive World and Its Transforma-*

tions. Ithaca, N. Y.: Cornell University Press, 1953. Ithaca: Cornell University Press, 1957. Paperback.

**Ruesch, Jurgen, and Gregory Bateson. *Communication: The Social Matrix of Psychiatry*. New York: Norton, 1951.

**Sapir, Edward. *Language: An Introduction to the Study of Speech*. New York: Harcourt, Brace, 1921. New York: Harcourt, Brace (HB7). Paperback.

**———. *Culture, Language and Personality: Selected Essays*, ed. David G. Mandelbaum. Berkeley: University of California Press, 1949. Paperback.

**Sebeok, Thomas A., Alfred S. Hayes, and Mary Catherine Bateson, eds. *Approaches to Semiotics*. The Hague: Mouton, 1964.

**Southwick, Charles H., ed. *Primate Social Behavior: An Enduring Problem*. Princeton: Van Nostrand, 1963. Paperback.

Steichen, Edward, ed. *The Family of Man*. New York: Museum of Modern Art, 1955. New York: Pocket Books, 1958 (GC51). Paperback.

**Teilhard de Chardin, Pierre. *The Phenomenon of Man*. Trans. Bernard Wall. New York: Harper, 1959. Paperback edition, New York and Evanston: Harper and Row, 1961 (TB83).

**Torre, Mottram, ed. *The Selection of Personnel for International Service*. Geneva and New York: World Federation for Mental Health, 1963.

Wagley, Charles, and Marvin Harris. *Minorities in the New World: Six Case Histories*. New York: Columbia University Press, 1959.

Wolf, Eric R. *Sons of the Shaking Earth*. Chicago: University of Chicago Press, 1959. Chicago: University of Chicago Press, 1962 (P90). Paperback.

Some Other Books by Margaret Mead

Mead, Margaret. *Coming of Age in Samoa.* New York: Morrow, 1928. New York: New American Library, 1949 (MP418). Paperback.

———. *Growing Up in New Guinea.* New York: Morrow, 1930. New York: New American Library, 1953 (MD255). Paperback.

———. *Sex and Temperament in Three Primitive Societies.* New York: Morrow, 1935. New York: New American Library, 1950 (MP370). Paperback.

———. *And Keep Your Powder Dry.* New York: Morrow, 1942.

———. *Male and Female.* New York: Morrow, 1949. New York: New American Library, 1955 (MP369). Paperback.

———, ed. *Cultural Patterns and Technical Change.* New York: New American Library, 1955 (MT346). Paperback.

———. *New Lives for Old: Cultural Transformation—Manus, 1928–1953.* New York: Morrow, 1956. New York: New American Library, 1961 (MT324). Paperback.

———. *An Anthropologist at Work: Writings of Ruth Benedict.* Boston: Houghton Mifflin, 1959.

———. *People and Places.* Cleveland and New York: World Publishing, 1959. New York: Bantam Books, 1963 (HP42). Paperback.

———, and Frances C. Macgregor. *Growth and Culture: A Photographic Study of Balinese Childhood.* New York: Putnam, 1951.

Some Publications by Anthropologists Interviewed in this Book

The books and articles listed here were selected from among their authors' writings because they are related to the kinds of things they talked about in their interviews. Some have been published in paperback editions; most of them you will be able to find in a larger library which has a section on anthropology.

Arensberg, Conrad M. *The Irish Countryman.* New York: Macmillan, 1937. Reissued 1959, Gloucester, Mass.: Smith.

———. "The Community as Object and as Sample," *American Anthropologist,* Vol. 63, No. 2 (1961), 241–64.

———, and Arthur H. Niehoff. *Introducing Social Change: A Manual for Americans Overseas.* Chicago: Aldine, 1964.

Bennett, Wendell C., and Junius B. Bird. *Andean Culture History,* 2d and rev. ed. American Museum Science Books. Garden City, N. Y.: Natural History Press, 1964 (B9). Paperback.

Bird, Junius B. "The Archeology of Pategonia." In *Handbook of South American Indians,* Vol. I, ed. Julian H. Steward. Washington: Smithsonian Institution, Bureau of American Ethnology, Bulletin 143, 1946, pp. 17–24.

———. "Art and Life in Old Peru: An Exhibition," *Curator,* Vol. 5, No. 2 (1961), 145–210.

Bunzel, Ruth L. *The Pueblo Potter: A Study of Creative Imagination in Primitive Art.* Columbia University Contributions to Anthropology, 8. New York: Columbia University Press, 1929.

———. *Chichicastenango: A Guatemalan Village.* Publications of the American Ethnological Society, 22. Locust Valley, N. Y.: Augustin, 1952.

Conklin, Harold C. "Hanunóo Color Categories," *Southwestern Journal of Anthropology,* Vol. 11, No. 4 (1955), 339–44.

———. "Maling, A Hanunóo Girl from the Philippines," and "A Day in Parina." In *In the Company of Man,* ed. Joseph B. Casagrande. New York: Harper, 1960, pp. 101–25. Paperback edition, New York: Harper and Row, 1964.

———. "Ethnogenealogical Method." In *Explorations in Cultural Anthropology: Essays in Honor of George Peter Murdock,* ed. Ward H. Goodenough. New York: McGraw-Hill, 1964, pp. 25–55.

Dole, Gertrude E., and Robert L. Carneiro, eds. *Essays in the Science of Culture in Honor of Leslie A. White.* New York: Crowell, 1960.

PUBLICATIONS BY ANTHROPOLOGISTS

Ekholm, Gordon F. "The Archeology of Northern and Western Mexico." In *The Maya and Their Neighbors*. New York: Appleton–Century, 1940, pp. 320–30.

———. "Excavations at Tampico and Panuco in the Huasteca, Mexico, "*Anthropological Papers of The American Museum of Natural History*," Vol. 38, Pt. 5, 1944, 319–512.

———. "Transpacific Contacts." In *Prehistoric Man in the New World*, Jesse D. Jennings and Edward Norbeck, eds., Chicago: University of Chicago Press, 1964, pp. 489–510.

Fairservis, Walter A., Jr. *The Origins of Oriental Civilization*. New York: New American Library, 1959 (MP445). Paperback.

———. *The Ancient Kingdoms of the Nile*. New York: New American Library, 1962 (MT460). Paperback.

Freed, Stanley A. "Changing Washo Kinship," *Anthropological Records*, Vol. 14, No. 6 (1960), 345–418.

———. "Fictive Kinship in a North Indian Village," *Ethnology*, Vol. 2, No. 1 (1963), 86–103.

———, and Ruth S. Freed. "The Persistence of Aboriginal Ceremonies among the Washo Indians." In "The Washo Indians of California and Nevada," *Anthropological Papers of the University of Utah*, Vol. 67, 1963, 25–40.

Fried, Morton H. *Fabric of Chinese Society*. New York: Praeger, 1953.

———. "On the Evolution of Social Stratification and the State." In *Culture in History: Essays in Honor of Paul Radin*, ed. Stanley Diamond. New York: Columbia University Press, 1960, pp. 713–31.

———, ed. *Readings in Anthropology*, 2 vols. Vol. I, *Physical Anthropology, Linguistics, and Archeology;* Vol. II, *Cultural Anthropology*. New York: Crowell, 1959. Paperback.

Gifford, Philip C. "Museum Materials on Television," *Curator*, Vol. 2, No. 4 (1959), 356–63.

———, and Joseph A. Nocera. "A Restored African Headdress," *Curator*, Vol. 5, No. 3 (1962), 245–52.

Greenberg, Joseph H. "Historical Linguistics and Unwritten Languages." In *Anthropology Today*, ed. A. L. Kroeber. Chicago: University of Chicago Press, 1953, pp. 265–86. Paperback edition, *Anthropology Today: Selections*, ed. Sol Tax. Chicago: University of Chicago Press, 1962 (P105), pp. 236–57.

———. *Essays in Linguistics*. Chicago: University of Chicago Press, 1957. Paperback edition, University of Chicago Press, 1964 (P119).

———, ed. *Universals of Language: Report of a Conference Held April 13–15, 1961*. Cambridge: M.I.T. Press, 1963.

Mencher, Joan. "Growing Up in South Malabar," *Human Organization*, Vol. 22, No. 1 (1963), 54–65.

Shapiro, Harry L. *The Heritage of the Bounty*. New York: Simon and Schuster, 1936. Paperback edition, rev. with a new postscript, Natural History Library. Garden City, N. Y.: Doubleday, 1962 (N23).

———. *Race Mixture*. Paris: Unesco, 1953. Distributed by the Columbia University Press. Paperback.

———, ed. *Man, Culture, and Society*. New York: Oxford University Press, 1956. Paperback edition, Oxford University Press (GB32).

———. "The History and Development of Physical Anthropology," *American Anthropologist*, Vol. 61, No. 3 (1959), 371–79.

———. *The Jewish People: A Biological History*. Paris: Unesco, 1960. Distributed by the Columbia University Press. Paperback.

Solecki, Ralph. "Early Man and Changing Sea Levels, Poplar Island, Maryland," *American Antiquity*, Vol. 27, No. 2 (1961), 234–36.

———. "New Anthropological Discoveries at Shanidar, Northern Iraq," *Transactions of the New York Academy of Sciences*, Ser. 2, Vol. 23, No. 8 (1961), 690–99.

Strong, William Duncan. "Anthropological Theory and Archaeological Fact." In *Essays in Anthropology Presented to A. L. Kroeber*, ed. Robert H. Lowie. Berkeley: University of California Press, 1936, pp. 359–70.

———. "Historical Approach in Anthropology." In *Anthropology Today*, ed. A. L. Kroeber. Chicago: University of Chicago Press, 1953, pp. 386–97.

———. "Original Peopling of the Americas." In *Encyclopedia of American History*, rev. and enl. ed., ed. Richard B. Morris. New York: Harper, 1961, pp. 3–13.

Turnbull, Colin M. *The Forest People*. New York: Simon and Schuster, 1961. Paperback edition, American Museum Science Books. Garden City, N.Y.: Natural History Press, 1962 (N27).

———. *The Lonely African*. New York: Simon and Schuster, 1962. Paperback edition, New York: Doubleday, 1963 (A374).

———. *The Peoples of Africa*. New York and Cleveland: World Publishing, 1962.

Wagley, Charles. *Amazon Town: A Study of Man in the Tropics*. New York: Macmillan, 1953. Paperback edition, with a new epilogue, New York: Knopf, 1964.

———. "Champukwi of the Village of Tapirs (Brazil)." In *In the Company of Man*, ed. Joseph B. Casagrande. New York: Harper, 1960, pp. 397–415. New York: Harper and Row, 1964. Paperback.

———. *An Introduction to Brazil*. New York: Columbia University Press, 1963.

Glossary

ABORIGINAL CULTURE. The traditional culture of a people before contact with one of the high civilizations, e.g. North American Indian cultures before the coming of European settlers.

ACCESSION. The formal process of adding an object or a group of objects to a museum collection.

ACCULTURATE. The process of acculturation by which one way of life, a culture, is passed from one people to another; the process of becoming adapted to a new way of life.

AMULET. A magical object, a charm, often ornamented, intended to protect the wearer against danger or to provide strength or good fortune.

ANTHROPOLOGY. The science of man. Contemporary branches include archeology, cultural anthropology, social anthropology, physical anthropology, linguistics, applied anthropology, etc.

ANTHROPOLOGY, APPLIED. The branch of anthropology concerned with the application of ideas and methods of anthropology to practical problems such as public health, urban resettlement, education, etc.

ANTHROPOLOGY, CULTURAL. The branch of anthropology concerned with the analysis and comparison of patterns of learned behavior and techniques of mastering the natural world in different cultures.

ANTHROPOLOGY, PHYSICAL. The branch of anthropology concerned with the biological study of man, including the historical development of the human species, human genetics, the differentiation of races and race mixture, anthropometry (*q.v.*), and the comparative study of man and other species.

ANTHROPOLOGY, SOCIAL. The branch of anthropology concerned with the analysis and comparison of forms of organization in society, especially in primitive societies.

ANTHROPOMETRY. The branch of physical anthropology concerned with measurement, including measurements taken both on human skeletons and on living persons, such as head form, stature, bodily proportions, skin, hair, and eye color, and other quantitative and qualitative measurements.

ARCHEOLOGY. The branch of anthropology concerned with the reconstruction of man's past mainly through the study of fossils, artifacts, art forms, settlement and burial sites, techniques of production, and often inferred social and cultural forms.

ARTIFACT. Any object made by human hands or, today, manufactured by a machine, e.g. a tool, a pot, a weapon, clothing, furniture, a tool to make a tool.

BARK CLOTH. Fabric made from the bark of some trees.

BLOOD FEUD. The practice of the family, clan, or community of a victim taking over responsibility for avenging his murder by killing some member of the killer's family, clan, or community.

CANTOMETRICS. The branch of anthropology concerned with the comparative analysis of song types within and in different cultures.

CARBON-14 DATING. A method of dating archeological specimens—fossils, bones, artifacts, etc.—by measuring the disintegration of radioactive carbon (C 14).

CASE. In a museum, the glass-walled container used for displaying specimens.

CATALOGUE. In a museum, the register of specimens and collections in which information is recorded about each object, such as when and how it was acquired, where it came from, what it is, etc.

CIVILIZATION. High or complex culture characterized by such techniques as metallurgy, irrigation, and scripts, and by such institutions as cities, complex political organization, class or caste divisions in society, etc.

COLLECTION. A group of material objects that enter or are kept in a museum as a unit for purposes of scientific research. For example, the Eskimo collection comprises all the specimens on display or in storage in the museum for the purpose of studying Eskimo cultures.

CULTURAL ANTHROPOLOGY. *See* anthropology, cultural.

CULTURAL EVOLUTION. The process of the development and elaboration of man's learned behaviors transmitted from one generation to the next by teaching throughout human history.

CULTURE. The subject matter of cultural anthropology (*q.v.*). Culture is the patterned and learned behavior of all human beings. A culture is the way of life of a specific people.

CURATOR. A scientist in charge of a museum collection or concerned with some special branch of knowledge in a museum.

DIFFUSION. The process by which ideas, beliefs, objects, or institutions, or any aspect of these (i.e. a culture trait) passes from one people to another.

DIG. An archeological site or excavation (*q.v.*).

DIORAMA. A reconstructed scene, at least partly three-dimensional, showing figures in a naturalistic setting. A diorama may be made on any scale—life-size (e.g. birds in their woodland setting) or miniaturized (e.g. a whole village scene in which men, animals, houses, trees, and all objects are proportionally reduced in size).

DISSERTATION. An essay, based on individual research, presented by a candidate for an academic degree (e.g. Ph.D.), as partial evidence of his knowledge of and training in some subject.

ECOLOGY. The study of the relationships between living organisms and their total natural environment. For man, the study of the human relationship to the natural and the man-made environment.

ETHNOGRAPHY. The descriptive study of a particular living, ongoing culture.

ETHNOLOGY. The comparative study of living, ongoing cultures, based on ethnographic studies of all the cultures included in a particular set of comparisons.

EXCAVATION. For the archeologist, the site where he is carrying on his field research, recovering the artifacts of a past culture or reconstructing an ancient village, religious center, burial ground, etc.

EXPEDITION. A field trip taken for a special scientific purpose, e.g. to study the life of a primitive people, or to recover the remains of a past civilization, or to collect specimens for a museum.

EXTENDED FAMILY. Kin related through a man or a woman living together as a group. One type of extended family consists of a man, his wife, his unmarried sons and daughters, his married sons and their wives and unmarried children, their married sons and their wives, etc.

FELLOW. An advanced student or a professional man or woman who has a grant to study or to do special research or other scientific work in a university, a museum, etc.

FIELD. An area of knowledge. Also an area of observation, the location where a scientist carries out observations or other forms of research, e.g. where an anthropologist makes his studies as a field worker.

FIELD SITE. The place where a scientist is carrying on research in a natural setting; the place where the archeologist is making an excavation (*q.v.*) or the anthropologist is studying a culture.

FIELD TRIP. A trip to carry out research in a natural setting, an expedition (*q.v.*).

FIELDWORK. The work done by a scientist in carrying out his research on an expedition (*q.v.*).

FOSSIL. Any hardened remains or traces of plant or animal life of some earlier geological period, preserved in earth or rock formations.

GENETICS, HUMAN. The study of the biological process of inheritance in man.

GRANT. Money from a fund given to a person or an institution for some special purpose, e.g. to do research as a fellow (*q.v.*), or to go on an expedition (*q.v.*), or to write up scientific work.

HABITAT. The locality or area in which a plant or animal

is found. The natural setting in which a people live.

HORTICULTURAL. Related to methods of working the soil and growing food with simple hand tools only, e.g. the hoe or the digging stick but not the plow. Primitive peoples who practice horticulture, in distinction to plow agriculture, are sometimes called "gardeners."

KINESICS. The branch of anthropology concerned with the comparative study of regularities in nonverbal behavior and the patterning of gesture.

KINSHIP. Relationships by blood or marriage. The study of kinship systems, i.e. of the formal patterning of family relationships recognized in a culture, is one important part of the study of social organization (*q.v.*).

LINGUISTICS. The branch of anthropology concerned with the analysis and comparative study of language, particularly spoken language without scripts of their own.

METHODOLOGY. A system of procedures regularly used for obtaining scientific results in some field of knowledge.

MONOGRAPH. A book or an article written for scientific purposes about one particular subject, e.g. a cultural study of a tribe.

MONTESSORI METHOD. A method of teaching young children that originated in the work of an Italian educator, Maria Montessori.

NATURAL SCIENCE. *See* science, natural.

NEANDERTHAL, CLASSICAL. A form of Neanderthal man with a low vaultage skull and certain cold-adaptive traits (heavy brows, etc.)

NEANDERTHAL, PROGRESSIVE. A form with a high vaultage skull and lacking some of the extreme traits of the cold-adaptive form.

NEANDERTHAL MAN. A form of man, *Homo neanderthalensis,* who lived *ca.* 100,000 to 50,000 years ago and whose remains have been found in Europe and the Middle East. This pre-Homo sapiens form of man had many variations and has been divided into different subgroups.

NEOLITHIC. Related to the Neolithic or New Stone Age, i.e. the prehistoric period when man gradually changed from a food-gatherer to a food-producer by domesticating plants and animals and began to live in more permanent settlements. "Neolithic" may be applied also to the cultures of contemporary primitive peoples whose economy and material culture has resemblances to those of man in the Neolithic Age.

NUCLEATED GROUP. A group of people living not in scattered homes but in a cluster, as in a hamlet.

ORNITHOLOGY. The branch of zoology dealing with the scientific study of birds.

PERUVIAN MONTAÑA. The dense tropical rain forest area in Peru, extending eastward from the slopes of the Andes.

PHYSICAL ANTHROPOLOGY. *See* anthropology, physical.

PHYSICAL SCIENCES. *See* science, physical.

PRIMITIVE MAN. Used in two different ways: (1) to refer to early man, i.e. prehistoric or ancient man; and (2) to refer to contemporary men living in primitive societies, i.e. comparatively small, simple societies without written languages of their own, lacking the characteristics of civilization (*q.v.*)

SAGO. A dry, mealy material or granulated paste, a starchy food that is prepared from the pith of various palm trees.

SCIENCE, NATURAL. Includes all the sciences except the social sciences (*q.v.*); a more inclusive term than physical science (*q.v.*).

SCIENCE, PHYSICAL. The group of sciences that deal with inanimate matter or energy, e.g. physics or chemistry.

SCIENCE, SOCIAL. The group of sciences that deal with the organized life of man, such as sociology (*q.v.*), social psychology, economics, or anthropology (*q.v.*), and by extension, that are concerned with the social life of other living organisms.

SEANCE. A meeting of a group of people for the purpose of communication with the supernatural (*q.v.*), usually conducted by a leader who is believed to have special access to the supernatural.

SEMIOTICS. The study of all forms of communication, verbal and nonverbal, grouped together. Includes linguistics (*q.v.*), kinesics (*q.v.*), etc.

SETTLEMENT PATTERN. The form of a people's living arrangements, with reference especially to the organization of space, as in rural and urban living, cities and villages, scattered farms or homesteads.

SILICA GEL. A chemical drying agent used in the wet tropics to protect equipment from the effects of moisture.

SITE. *See* field site.

SOCIAL ANTHROPOLOGY. *See* anthropology, social.

SOCIAL ORGANIZATION. The ordered relations of different parts of a society, studied from the point of view of ways of grouping people, e.g. by kinship, class or caste, political relations, economic relations, etc.

SOCIAL SCIENCE. *See* science, social.

SOCIOLOGY. The science that deals with the problems, the historical development, and the forms of organization of people living together. Historically, sociology has been concerned with social life in complex cultures or civilization (*q.v.*), and social anthropology (*q.v.*) has been concerned with primitive peoples, but this distinction no longer holds.

SPECIMEN. A sample of a class of things. In a museum, a single item in a collection (*q.v.*), typical of its kind.

SUPERNATURAL. Related to or characterized by what is outside the natural order.

TRIBE. A group usually living within a definite area, speaking a common language, having a unifying social organization (*q.v.*), and sharing a way of life, a culture (*q.v.*).

WARP. In weaving, the parallel foundation threads running lengthwise in the loom.

WEFT. In weaving, the threads carried back and forth at right angles and over and under the warp (*q.v.*) to form a fabric.

XINGU RIVER. A river in central Brazil, pronounced *shin-gōō′*.

Index